IMAGES
*of Aviation*

# IN CORNISH
# SKIES

Captain Percival Phillips, DFC, MSM, formed the Cornish Aviation Company in May 1924, with its base at St Austell. His aircraft, mostly pillar-box red Avro 504Ks, became famous across the country as Phillips and his pilots toured Britain during the summer seasons with their amazing stunt-flying and wing-walking acts. The company also offered short joy-rides to members of the public, and these were tremendously popular: between 1924 and 1931 Phillips himself took no fewer than 55,100 passengers up, a truly formidable work-rate. (*Author's collection*)

IMAGES
*of Aviation*

# IN CORNISH
# SKIES

Peter London

TEMPUS

First published 2000
Copyright © Peter London, 2000

Tempus Publishing Limited
The Mill, Brimscombe Port,
Stroud, Gloucestershire, GL5 2QG

ISBN 0 7524 2101 8

Typesetting and origination by
Tempus Publishing Limited
Printed in Great Britain by
Oakland Book Services

When the Second World War broke out, the elderly Westland Wallaces of G Flight, No.1 Anti-Aircraft Co-operation Unit were working with No.6 Heavy-Anti Aircraft Artillery Practice Camp, situated at Cleave, near Bude on Cornwall's northernmost coastline. The Wallaces were used to tow targets for the benefit of Cleave Camp's trainee anti-aircraft gunners. Here, the ground crew take a moment for a group photograph during early 1940. The winch winding mechanism used to deploy the targets is visible aft of the aircraft's rear cockpit. (*Bill Young*)

# Contents

# Acknowledgements

I am very pleased to acknowledge with many thanks the generous help and support I have received from the following people and institutions, which has enabled this project to come to fruition: Air-Britain, Bob Andrew, Peter R. Arnold, Chris Ashworth, David Barnes, G. Perry Bauchman, Tim Bishop, Paddy Bradley, British International Helicopters, Jack Bruce, Denys Bryant, Brian Butcher, Keith Butcher, Mrs J. Church, Barry Cole, Ian Collett, Laurie Cunningham, Dennis Ellery, Frank Gibson, Peter H.T. Green, Helston Folk Museum, Gerry Holder, Imperial War Museum, Mike Ingham, Mrs Vivienne Jenkins, Chris Julian, Dennis Keam, Rod Knight, Keith Lee, Stuart Leslie, Paul Longthorp, Frank Marshall, Malcolm McCarthy, Fred Motley, Bob Partridge, Public Archives of Canada, John Rapson, Mike Retallack, Paul Richards, Royal Cornwall Polytechnic Society Research Project (Peter Gilson), Royal Naval Air Station Culdrose, Keith Saunders, Peter Seaborn, Ian Stratford, Andy Thomas, Barry Venn, Reg Watkiss, Peter Wearne, Mike Whittaker, Bill Young, 247 Squadron Association.

This book is for my friend Barry Saxton, a keen follower of Cornish matters, who has for twenty-five years put up with my keen interest in aeroplanes!

All reasonable measures have been taken to identify the sources of the photographs that appear in this book. However, because of the passage of time, as well as the uncertain origins of some of the photographs, it may be that in a few instances use has accidentally been made without correct acknowledgement of the originator. Please accept my apologies if your name has not been included within the list of acknowledgements above. Should such a situation arise and the publisher is notified accordingly, I would be pleased to amend this in any future editions of this book.

Perranporth Gliding (and Flying) School's beautiful bright yellow Schleicher Ka.7, CMZ *Spirit of Cornwall* (BGA 1664) photographed on a glorious day at the airfield during the late 1990s. A car tyre is used to prevent the wind, usually a feature at the clifftop location, from rocking the aircraft. CMZ is about to get a lift from the Club's aero-tow, Pawnee 235D G-BFEW. (*Author's collection*)

# Introduction

Cornwall's first flights were made at Penzance on 23 July 1910 by the pioneer airman Claude Grahame-White, who piloted a Farman. A further aeronautical visit, by French pilot Henri Salmet, took place in June 1912, while Briton Gustav Hamel called during September 1913, both men bringing Bleriots. During April 1914, Salmet returned to the county while in June, Lord John Carbery gave flying exhibitions at Redruth, using a Morane.

August 1914 marked the outbreak of the First World War. During February 1915, Germany announced a policy of indiscriminate submarine warfare in all British waters. This led to the construction of airship stations around a large proportion of Britain's coastline, controlled by the Royal Naval Air Service (RNAS), in order to help protect British and Allied merchant shipping from German U-boats. Cornwall's Lizard peninsula was a strategically favourable location for such a site and accordingly, Royal Naval Air Station Mullion was established there during June 1916. Several airship mooring-out stations subordinate to Mullion were later constructed, at nearby Bochym Wood, at Langford Barton just south of Bude, Laira (Plymouth), Toller (Bridport) and Upton (Poole).

Mullion operated Coastal ('C') Class airships – C.2, C.9, C.10, C.22, and C.23a all flew from the station. Also employed were smaller Submarine Scout Zero (SSZ) Class airships: Numbers 14, 15, 25, 27, 40, 42, 45, 47, 49 and 75 served at various times between July 1917 and December 1918. The strength of the airships was their deterrent value and, though many long patrols were flown, few incidents were recorded. The site of a bomb-laden assailant was usually enough to make a U-boat submerge smartly but the airships were successful in damaging several submarines and contributing to the sinking of others. The crew of Mullion-based Coastal Class C.9 managed to destroy a U-boat without any aid from surface vessels.

During the early part of 1918 a modified SSZ Class appeared, designed at Mullion by a group of officers there – the so-called *Mullion Twin*, or SSE.2. The new airship was powered by two 75-hp Rolls Royce Hawk engines and was delivered in March 1918. SSE.2 became the basis for a new category of airship, the SST Class. Two larger Coastal Star (C*) Class airships also operated in Cornwall for a time.

Mullion became a home for aircraft of the RNAS when Sopwith $1\frac{1}{2}$ Strutters and de Havilland DH.6s arrived to carry out further U-boat patrols. RNAS stations were formed too at Newlyn and Padstow, and on Tresco. RNAS Newlyn/Land's End was established in January 1917, operating Short 184 floatplanes against the submarines. RNAS Tresco, a twenty-acre site, was operational by the end of February 1917 employing Curtiss H.12 and later Felixstowe F.3 flying-boats. A fifty-acre airfield was prepared near Padstow and the station commissioned in March 1918 as RNAS Padstow/Crugmeer, flying DH.6s and DH.9s on inshore patrols.

Military aviation left Cornwall soon after the war, though the RAF made a brief return when their Seaplane Development Flight passed through Newlyn and the Isles of Scilly in August 1922. During the immediate post-war years, aeroplanes were still a rarity in the county. However, visits to Cornwall by the aerial joy-riding concerns that grew after the war brought aviation to the people there. In fact one of the leading such enterprizes was the Cornwall Aviation Company, founded in May 1924 by Captain Percival Phillips, a resident of St Austell. The company provided the opportunity for the public to witness truly astonishing stunt-flying as well as wing-walking performed without any safety equipment, and to experience short joy-rides. Phillips' first aircraft was vivid red Avro 504K G-EBIZ. At first the concern plied the Cornish resorts – Newquay, Fowey and Penzance were all visited – but in later years Phillips' growing fleet ranged far and wide, using improvised landing-strips across the country. Sir Alan Cobham also visited Cornwall, using his National Aviation Day Displays circus to promote air-mindedness and civil aviation through displays of different types and forms of aircraft, passenger flights and stunts. The Circus toured the county twice during 1932, and also in 1933, 1934 and 1935. As time passed, however, the excitement of the shows palled, for the public became familiar with such events and the barnstormers faded from the scene.

The first firm to provide a commercial passenger service to Cornwall was Provincial Airways, which in April 1934 opened a route between Plymouth and Hayle. By August, Provincial's service included another Cornish stop, at Newquay, the landing strip being located at Trebelzue Big Field, also used by Cobham. However, Provincial went into liquidation in September 1935. On 15 September 1937, Channel Air Ferries commenced a service between the newly-established Land's End (St Just) aerodrome to the tiny airfield situated on St Mary's, employing DH.84 Dragons. During May 1938 that company started a service from Land's End to Plymouth and on to Bristol, as well as a more extensive route serving Brighton, the Isle of Wight, Bournemouth, Bristol and Cardiff. In March 1939, Channel was formally merged into the new carrier Great Western & Southern Air Lines, but the services continued. On 8 May, Western Airways opened a route from Swansea to Penzance via Barnstaple and Newquay. At Newquay, Western used the northern (smaller) portion of Trebelzue Big Field, which by then had become an AA Landing Ground.

Further small airfields appeared in Cornwall toward the end of the decade. During 1937 a fifty-two-acre site was laid out just south of St Merryn on the north coast, the controlling authority of which was St Merryn Aerodrome Ltd, with a registered office in London. A further field at Treligga, $1\frac{1}{2}$ miles west of Delabole, was established as a gliding site and was used by the newly-formed Cornwall Gliding Club. Gliding was also carried out at Summercourt, Rosenannon Downs, St Wenn and, occasionally, from the beach at Penzance. After preparations started during March 1939, an airstrip near Ludgvan, just north-east of Penzance, was opened to serve the town.

On 3 September 1939 Britain declared war on Germany. By then, the first military airfield in Cornwall since the First World War had been commissioned, at Cleave, four miles north of Bude on the cliff top near the village of Kilkhampton. The station was used by the target towing and drone aircraft of No.1 Anti-Aircraft Co-operation Unit, in conjunction with summer anti-aircraft co-operation and training camps. Cleave was populated by Wallaces and Queen Bees and later by Henleys and Hurricanes. During October 1939 RAF St Eval opened, situated around five miles north-east of Newquay. St Eval's planning had commenced during 1937, as the feeling grew that anti-submarine work might once more be necessary around the Cornish coastline. St Eval was designed to accommodate two Coastal Command general reconnaissance squadrons, though as the war progressed the station often became populated by great numbers and varieties of aircraft.

In December 1939 the Admiralty requisitioned 550 acres of land between St Merryn and St Ervan, around three miles south-west of Padstow, for a new Naval Air Station for training purposes. Construction began early in 1940 and subsumed the civil airfield established there in 1937. The station was commissioned on 10 August 1940 as RNAS St Merryn, taking the ship's name HMS *Vulture*. During March 1940, meanwhile, a further 260 acres of land had been acquired by the Admiralty at the pre-war gliding site of Treligga in order to provide an air-to-ground firing range. Three emergency landing strips were placed around Treligga, which became a satellite of St Merryn and was named HMS *Vulture II*.

In June 1940 France fell and Cornwall became vulnerable to attacks by the Luftwaffe, being bombed for the first time on 5 July. Eight days later the RAF's No.10 Group was formed and St Eval became a Sector Airfield responsible for the control of all aircraft within its area, including the newly-arrived Spitfires of No.234 Squadron and No.238 Squadron's Hurricanes. Between March and May 1941 three new fighter airfields were opened. An area four miles north-west of Redruth at Nancekuke Common, near Portreath on the north coast, was selected as the site for Cornwall's main fighter base. The station would be supported by two further new airfields, one at Perranporth, near Newquay, for the operation of day fighters, the other at Predannack on the Lizard for night fighters.

RAF Portreath opened on 7 March 1941, receiving 263 Squadron's Whirlwinds, followed by 152 Squadron's Spitfires and Hurricanes of 247 Squadron. RAF Perranporth commenced operations on 28 April 1941, located on the cliff top between St Agnes and Perranporth; its first occupants were 66 Squadron's Spitfire IIAs. In May 1941 RAF Predannack came into being, located south of Mullion village on the Lizard. No.247 Squadron arrived there in June, operating Hurricane IIAs, followed by a detachment of 600 Squadron, bringing night-fighter Beaufighters. Finally, in the same month as Predannack opened, a westernmost fighter outpost was established when St Mary's received six Hurricanes detached from 87 Squadron.

As the fight was taken to the enemy across the Channel, Blenheims flew from Cornwall to raid the French coast. By August 1941, Portreath sometimes controlled as many as seven fighter squadrons, these flying from Perranporth and Predannack as well as Portreath itself, as cover for the raiding bombers. In September 1941, the new Coastal Command airfield RAF Trebelzue opened, the former civilian Big Field having been requisitioned as a satellite for St Eval. For a time, Trebelzue acted as a nocturnal retreat for St Eval's aircraft, to avoid their destruction during air raids there. That autumn, Portreath commenced use as the starting point for long-range ferry flights of squadrons departing for North Africa and the Middle East, via Gibraltar and Malta. The possibility was considered of also employing Trebelzue for such work but the station was considered inadequate for the size of the task ahead. It was decided to build a new, larger station just to the east, retaining Trebelzue as a dispersal area.

Spring and summer 1942 at St Eval saw the arrival of Hudsons and Whitleys to boost efforts in the U-boat war. Over the summer, aircraft from the fighter airfields continued sweeps across northern France and mounted repeated convoy patrols. On 16 August, Predannack-based Liberator AM917/F of 120 Squadron attacked and damaged the U-89 with depth charges. This strike marked the beginning of Squadron Leader T.M. Bulloch's career in anti-submarine warfare; he became the most successful U-boat hunter in the RAF. Two days later, Bulloch severely damaged the U-653. On 19 August 1942 Operation *Jubilee* took place, and Portreath contributed to the air cover provided for the ill-fated Dieppe landings.

On 1 October a further Cornish airfield opened for business: RAF Davidstow Moor, situated two miles north-east of Camelford near the northern part of Bodmin Moor. Davidstow was the highest operational airfield in the United Kingdom at 970ft. Eighth Air Force B-17s and B-24s of 44th and 93rd BGs were the main occupants at first, staging between their East Anglian bases and European targets. Davidstow was later used by 19 Group Coastal Command. October at Portreath, Predannack and St Eval saw a considerable build-up of American aircraft as part of the effort in support of Operation *Torch*, the Allied invasion of Vichy French North Africa in November.

No.602 Squadron (Spitfire VCs) arrived at Perranporth in January 1943, while St Eval received 502 Squadron's Halifax IIs during February. On 24 February, the new airfield subsuming Trebelzue was named RAF St Mawgan. Portreath continued with ferry-flight work, which by then included Mosquitos and Liberators. At Predannack, 248 Squadron (Beaufighter VIC) was joined by 141 Squadron's nightfighter Beaufighters, for shipping strikes and Instep work against German anti-shipping aircraft. In March, Mosquitos of 307 *Lvov* Squadron arrived, the first Poles to serve at Predannack. April saw the arrival of Predannack's first full Mosquito Squadron, 264, for reconnaissance and maritime attack. In June, 295 Squadron (Halifax Vs) was detached to Portreath in readiness for Horsa tows to North Africa in support of Operation *Beggar*, the invasion of Sicily, and by August, St Mawgan's facilities had become fully available. At first, that station was used principally by Whitley glider-tugs of 297 Squadron, exercised with Horsas in preparation for Operation *Husky*, and by Air Transport Command, USAAF. By the autumn, St Mawgan was one of the busiest stations in the country, shipping hundreds of aircraft to North Africa and the Mediterranean.

Following Davidstow's use by the Eighth Air Force, 19 Group Coastal Command took control during the summer of 1943; anti-submarine work over The Bay of Biscay was commenced by Wellingtons. The final part of 1943 saw St Mawgan's ferry work decline somewhat, but from November, the airfield became a link in the BOAC North African route flown by camouflaged

DC-3s. Meanwhile, St Merryn's School of Air Combat commenced work during September. No.736 Squadron (Seafires) moved there, where it became one of the key parts of the new establishment. The School later employed Masters, Fireflies and Barracudas, and trifurcated into discrete training squadrons – 709 (ground attack instruction), 715 (a second air combat squadron) and 719 (weapon training). In September 1943, No.183 Squadron (Typhoon IA and IB) arrived at Perranporth, charged with attacking enemy shipping and airfields across the Channel. However, the Perranporth runways were found too short and the Typhoons transferred to Predannack in October. The following month, St Eval received two Leigh Light-equipped Wellington squadrons, 407 and 612. Portreath, meanwhile, had continued its Beaufighter anti-shipping strikes. During December Davidstow became responsible for air-sea rescue work when Warwicks detached from 280 Squadron arrived.

During 1944 St Mawgan continued to transit American aircraft, while Transport Command passenger flights commenced there in March. St Eval hosted Liberators on anti-submarine work from early 1944, while the Davidstow Warwicks continued their work. Portreath accommodated 248 Squadron from February, its Mosquitos flying strike operations. 206 Squadron (Fortress IIs and IIAs), moved to Davidstow during March, before transferring to St Eval and re-equipping with Liberator VIs. In April, 524 Squadron arrived at Davidstow with Wellington XIVs fitted with ASV and Leigh Lights, for anti E-boat patrols. During May the Beaufighters of 144 and 404 (RCAF) Squadrons were posted there, also in the anti-shipping role, being named 154 (GR) Wing.

No.235 Squadron (Beaufighters, later Mosquitos) had arrived at Portreath in April, forming 153 (GR) Wing with 248 Squadron as the build-up to D-Day continued. At Perranporth, 145 Free French Wing was created with three Spitfire squadrons, concentrating on Instep patrols. In March, 151 Squadron arrived at Predannack with Mosquitos and, by the end of April, a Predannack Spitfire IX Wing had formed from 1 and 165 Squadrons for further Insteps. In early June the Predannack Spitfire Wing provided cover for the huge invasion convoy gathering at Falmouth, lending support until it had reached France, after when enemy coastal radar installations, shipping, airfields and goods trains were attacked. Perranporth provided round-the-clock patrols until August, using Avengers and Swordfish, while Cornwall-based Beaufighters and Mosquitos co-operated in attacking German shipping. Anti U-boat patrols continued throughout the period and on 7 June a Liberator of 53 Squadron succeeded in damaging both the U-963 and the U-256 during the same mission. Two days following D-Day, a 224 Squadron Liberator flying from St Eval destroyed two U-boats, the U-629 and the U-373, within half an hour in separate low-level attacks.

After the summer of 1944, however, the pace of activity slowed. On 1 September Perranporth was reduced to Care and Maintenance status, followed by Davidstow on 26 September and St Mary's at the end of that month. At Predannack, the Wellingtons and Liberators left over the summer as U-boat activity reduced. St Eval's Liberators had departed by September, but Warwicks arrived to provide ASR cover. In November BOAC's operation left St Mawgan. Portreath lost its ASR Warwicks when 277 Squadron left in February 1945 and its operations room closed on 15 April. VE Day found Predannack with no Squadrons at all. Cleave was reduced to Care and Maintenance on 16 May. Predannack soldiered on until June 1946 when it too assumed Care and Maintenance status. Portreath's air traffic control facilities shut down on 9 October and in November Cleave closed. The following month Care and Maintenance status followed for Portreath, while Davidstow also closed. Perranporth was transferred to 44 Group during February 1946 but there were no further aircraft movements and the airfield closed in April. St Eval and St Mawgan continued, however, the latter becoming Transport Command's No.1 Diversion Centre for despatch of large aircraft to the Far East; that base also dealt with American and Canadian aircraft returning home, and later acted as an assembly point for aircraft destined for the rebuilding French Air Force. However, with these tasks complete, on 1 July 1947 St Mawgan too went to Care and Maintenance status, though it was subsequently used occasionally by civil operators. St Merryn continued as a Naval training establishment.

Great Western and Southern's civil passenger service between Land's End and St Mary's had continued almost uninterrupted throughout the war years, retaining DH.89s and, though the company was taken over by BEA on 1 February 1947, the service continued. Meanwhile, Island Air Services had been formed in June 1945 based at St Mary's, operating two Proctors over the following summer on pleasure and light transport flights. The Proctors and Consul of Patrick-Duval Aviation of Birmingham visited both Land's End and St Mary's to collect flowers during the early part of 1947. The summer of 1949 saw a brief operation when Aquila Airways flew charter flights carrying holidaymakers between Falmouth and St Mary's, using civilianized Sunderlands. During 1949 and 1950, the Plymouth and District Aero Club adopted the Trebelzue end of St Mawgan for charter and pleasure flying. FinGland's Airways Ltd commenced a tourist route between Ringway and St Mawgan in June 1950 employing Ansons, but the Air Ministry repossessed St Mawgan in 1951. Commercial services over the summers of 1951 and 1952 therefore used derequisitioned Perranporth. Murray Chown Aviation flew between Trebelzue, Perranporth, Land's End and St Mary's during the 1950 season, followed by services from Perranporth covering Staverton, Cardiff, St Mary's and Guernsey during the 1951 and 1952 seasons. BEA's Land's End-St Mary's service proved very popular and DH89s continued in use, the last BEA service to operate Rapides. The BEA route was extremely busy, sometimes making over twenty round trips each day during the high season. Starways Airlines opened a service between Liverpool and St Mawgan in June 1959, by when the Air Ministry had become flexible regarding the limited use of St Mawgan for civil purposes. Starways opened a further holiday route later that month between Liverpool, Exeter and St Mawgan, flown each Saturday using DC-3s.

The 1960s witnessed a great growth in commercial aviation in Cornwall. Competition was stern and traffic was based on the holiday season. In March 1961 Mayflower Air Services was formed at Plymouth; its first flight, to St Mary's, was made on 13 June. The company made successful inroads into the tourist trade and more routes were added, terminating at St Mary's from Bristol, Cardiff and Newquay. During July 1963, however, Mayflower's DH.89 G-AHLM crashed at St Mary's and the pilot, who also owned the company, was badly burned. Scillonian Air Services, established in 1962 to connect St Mary's with Gatwick, acquired Mayflower in 1963. Meanwhile, during 1962 a portion of RAF St Mawgan had become known as Newquay Airport (RAF St Mawgan), and a modest civil terminal was built. During that year, Exeter-based Westpoint Aviation opened a service between Newquay, Exeter and Heathrow. In May 1964, the renamed Westpoint, by then known as British Westpoint, took over Scillonian. During that summer, British Westpoint continued services to St Mary's from Bristol, Cardiff, Exeter, Newquay and Plymouth. That year too, BEA finally replaced its aged Rapides with Sikorsky S-61N helicopters; on 2 May G-ASNL flew the first scheduled service from Land's End. BEA's last three Rapides, G-AGSH, 'HKU and 'JCL, passed to British Westpoint. At Penzance a heliport was opened on 1 September 1964, designed by BEA, and the S-61s relocated.

The year 1965 witnessed the first flights by British Midland Airways between Castle Donington and Newquay. In May 1966 British Westpoint ceased trading, but a new company emerged, Scillonia Airways, employing Rapides between Newquay, Land's End and St Mary's. By July 1966, as well as Viscounts British Eagle was using BAC 1-11s on its Newquay route, the first commercial jets to operate in Cornwall. Scillonia's financial position deteriorated until its services were suspended, the assets of the company finally being auctioned off. In May 1969, Dan-Air commenced a Gatwick-Newquay service, but the service lasted only that season. The year 1969 also saw the emergence of Westward Airways, which in July began a daily Newquay-Plymouth-Gatwick-eathrow service. However, by the autumn of 1970 that company too had ceased trading.

Though many of Cornwall's military airfields had closed shortly after the war, St Merryn and St Eval continued. St Merryn supported Naval operational flying training, employing Firefly FR.Is, Barracudas and some Seafire IIIs, while its School of Naval Air Warfare provided advanced flying training. St Eval was retained as the area's Coastal Command station and, in January 1947, No.203 Squadron arrived, converting from Liberators to Lancaster GR.3s. On 17 April 1947 a

11

new Cornish naval airfield was commissioned, situated south-east of Helston: RNAS Culdrose (HMS *Seahawk*). Training duties commenced there, employing the Naval Instrument Flying Instructional Flight (Oxfords and Harvards) and later a Night Fighter Training Unit (Firefly NF.1s), as well as Ansons for AI radar training, together with 762 Squadron (also Ansons) for twin-engine conversion courses. The station managed the introduction into service of the Sea Hornet and received a number of units from St Merryn as the latter station began the run-down of its own comparatively modest training facilities.

In the meantime St Mawgan had been left to its own devices, apart from hosting occasional leisure and commercial flying. On 16 April 1951, however, the station re-opened and the School of Maritime Reconnaissance (SMR) formed there on Lancaster MR.3s; shortly afterwards, the Air Sea Warfare Development Unit arrived. Elsewhere, during November 1951 the Shackleton MR.1s of 220 Squadron arrived at St Eval, followed by 42 Squadron in June 1952 and 206 Squadron during September, also flying Shackleton MR.1s. By the summer of 1952 St Eval was one of the twelve Master Diversion Airfields in the UK. In January 1953 the first of 42 Squadron's Shackleton MR.2s arrived, while, on 1 July 1954, No.228 Squadron reformed at St Eval, also receiving Shackleton MR.2s. In November 1955 St Mawgan became the area's Master Diversion Airfield.

With the establishment of Culdrose, St Merryn's end came. Its runways were considered short by the mid-1950s, and in June 1955 it was reduced to Care and Maintenance, being closed by the Navy on 10 January 1956; Treligga closed later that year. Culdrose, meanwhile, had grown with the arrival of 702 Squadron, the Naval Jet Evaluation and Training Unit, the establishment of No.1 Naval Air Fighter School and subsequently of an Advanced Jet Flying School employing Attackers and Meteor T.7s. During August 1951, No.759 Squadron formed as No.1 Operational Flying School, part of the Naval Air Fighter School. Airborne Early Warning trials commenced during October 1951 by 778 Squadron, employing four Skyraider AEW.1s. In 1955 the Naval Observer and Air Signals School was formed. No.825 Squadron recommissioned on 4 July 1955, becoming Culdrose's first Gannet squadron, with eight AS.1 aircraft.

In December 1956 the Shackletons of 228 and 220 Squadrons moved from St Eval to St Mawgan, the station's first operational squadrons. No.220 flew the Shackleton MR.3, which was too heavy to take off from St Eval and required the longer runways of St Mawgan. In 1958, No.42 Squadron moved to St Mawgan while St Eval was degraded to Care and Maintenance status during March 1959. Work commenced on refurbishing Predannack as an overspill for Culdrose, which had been selected as the main helicopter training base for the Navy; the latter station also accommodated 831 Squadron, the Electronic Warfare Unit and, by 1959, the School of Aircraft Handling. In June 1959, 700H Squadron formed the Intensive Flying Trials Unit (IFTU) for the introduction into service of the Whirlwind HAS.7 at Culdrose, while in August 700G Squadron formed the IFTU there for the Gannet AEW.3. In April 1960, 700H Squadron formed the IFTU for the Wessex HAS.1 anti-submarine helicopter. No.700W (IFTU) Squadron took initial charge of the Westland Wasp into service while 700V (IFTU) introduced the Wessex HU.5. In 1967 the Wessex HAS.3 entered service following work-up by 700H (IFTU) Squadron at Culdrose during that year. In 1969 the Royal Navy began the introduction of the Sea King HAS.1 through 700S (IFTU). At St Mawgan meanwhile, the Shackletons continued maritime patrols until, in March 1965, No.201 Squadron left for Kinloss where it was joined by No.206 in July of that year. In exchange, St Mawgan received the Shackleton T.4s of the Maritime Operational Training Unit (MOTU). In October 1969, No.236 OCU took on charge its first Nimrod MR.1s at St Mawgan, its job to convert Shackleton crews to the incoming type.

Brymon Airways first came to Cornwall in September 1970, when Islander G-AXXJ flew charter flights to St Mary's and Land's End. Island Air Charter Ltd was formed at Land's End during the summer of 1970 with Islander G-AYCV, for charter work and pleasure flying. August 1971 saw the formation of V.H. Bellamy's Westward Airways (Land's End), while Brymon established a base at Newquay Airport in 1972. Over that summer, British Midland operated a London-Newquay service using Viscounts, while in September, British Airways Helicopters (BAH), successor to BEA Helicopters, acquired the Penzance-St Mary's route. In 1973 Brymon moved their centre of operations to Plymouth; by 1974 the company had introduced the de Havilland Canada DHC.6 Twin Otter, and in January 1977 took over the running of Newquay airport. During 1977, Brymon carried over 25,000 passengers on its Newquay-London flight alone. Viscount operations also grew at Newquay as the 1970s drew to an end; Alidair, Guernsey Air Lines and Jersey European Air Lines all ran services. In August 1981, Brymon accepted its first de Havilland Canada Dash 7. An additional BAH service was introduced in March 1983 when the Penzance-Tresco route via St Mary's was opened. By 1985 Brymon's Isles of Scilly connections ran to Bristol, Exeter, Newquay and Plymouth. In September, British Airways sold its helicopter subsidiary, the company being renamed British International Helicopters (BIH).

In March 1987 a passenger licence was granted to the Land's End-based company Skybus to operate a scheduled service connecting Land's End and St Mary's, and employing Islanders. Since then, Skybus routes have spread to cover Bristol, Exeter, Newquay and Plymouth; the company's base is still Land's End. In addition to passengers, freight, mail and local produce are carried. Islanders continue in use, along with Twin Otter G-BIHO, and during the busiest summer Saturdays as many as forty-five round trips are made between Land's End and St Mary's. In 1993 Brymon became wholly-owned by British Airways and began operating all its scheduled services as British Airways on 1 August. The company retains its Plymouth base but continues to fly from Newquay as the main commercial user there, a daily service running to London and Plymouth. BIH's parent company is now the Canadian Helicopter Corporation. The route is the only scheduled helicopter service in Britain and is the longest established such service in the world.

While the Cornish civil aviation scene was still growing, meanwhile, during May 1970, No.7 Squadron had reformed at St Mawgan flying Canberra TT.18s in the target facilities role, providing aircraft as low and fast targets to exercise radar and surface-to-air weapons procedures. During April 1971, No.42 Squadron began the conversion to Nimrod MR.1s for surveillance, anti-submarine warfare training and search-and-rescue duties, together with fishery protection and oil rig surveillance. St Mawgan's Nimrods were shared between 42 Squadron and 236 OCU. In September 1972 the Royal Naval Observer School returned to Culdrose, bringing No.750 Squadron equipped with Sea Princes (later Jetstream T.2s), while a dedicated Sea King Training Unit was formed there from 1972 until 1976 to instruct foreign aircrews. The station's 705 Squadron equipped with Gazelle HT.2s from March 1974 for initial helicopter training, while in September 771 Squadron arrived, providing a SAR capability, initially on Wessex but later using Sea Kings. Culdrose-based Squadrons served with distinction in the Falklands war while training continued to be the main activity on station and still is today.

During 1982, No.236 OCU's Nimrods transferred from St Mawgan to Kinloss, but 42 Squadron remained, participating in Operation *Corporate*. No.236 OCU returned with Nimrod MR.2s during October 1983 and, in the following year, 42 Squadron also converted to the MR.2. However, the early 1990s saw flying at St Mawgan reduce with the departure of the Nimrods, the last example of which left for Kinloss on 9 September 1992. By 1995 the station housed HQ Flight, 22 Squadron (Sea Kings), and the RAF's Sea King OCU. The Cornwall Air Ambulance and Trinity House Bölkows share a hangar there.

Currently, Culdrose accommodates three anti-submarine Squadrons – 810, 814 and 820 – while a fourth, 849, carries out an Airborne Early Warning role, all Squadrons operating various marks of the Sea King. In addition, 771 Squadron Sea King HAR.5s continue to provide SAR facilities for both military and civilian purposes, every day of the year, round the clock, within a radius of 200 nautical miles. During 1996, Hawks of the Fleet Requirements and Air Direction Unit (FRADU) relocated to Culdrose. The station's Squadrons participated in the NATO (later IFOR –Implementation Force) operations off Bosnia and in the second Gulf Crisis in January 1999. The station is still home to the School of Aircraft Handling (now the School of Flight Deck Operations) and Predannack continues to support training. The Merlin Intensive

Flying Trials Unit (700M Squadron) was commissioned on 1 December 1998 at Culdrose to bring into service the Navy's newest helicopter.

A number of airfields used for private flying have emerged in Cornwall since the war. The former RAF Perranporth had been adopted as a gliding base by youngsters from the ATC as far back as May 1945. Sporadic use followed, notably by the Plymouth and District Aero Club but in 1957 the Cornish Gliding (and Flying) Club arrived, formed by a group of ex-RAF wartime pilots, together with ex-instructors from both the RAF and ATC gliding schools. The Club is still very active, especially during the summer months. A number of gliders live at Perranporth, while aero-tows are by courtesy of Pawnee 235D G-BFEW. In Penwith, following the departure of BEA in 1964 Land's End airfield was run by the Land's End Aero Club. In addition, Westward Airways (Land's End) has operated a great variety of aircraft. Land's End also accommodates privately-owned aircraft. The present Land's End Flying Club employs the Cessna 152 and Cherokee 140, while Cessna FR.172F G-AWWU performs pleasure flights. Meanwhile, some three miles north-east of Bodmin, at Cardinham, a private flying airfield was established during the early 1970s by Mike Robertson, founder of the Trago Mills retail empire. The Cornwall Flying Club was founded at Bodmin, its early aircraft including Forney F-1As, Ercoupes and Aircoupes but currently, Cessnas are flown.

Cornwall is not of course an industrial centre but, remarkably, the county has seen the creation of several original aircraft types from the 1970s on, and two of particular interest. The Whittaker MW.2 Excalibur ultra-light was designed and built at Bodmin airfield between 1972 and 1976, but used St Mawgan for its first (and only) flight on 1 July 1976. Unfortunately the project was taken no further. The Trago Mills SAH-1 two-seat trainer was also designed and constructed at Bodmin, first flying there on 23 August 1983. Despite enjoying an outstanding performance and receiving many very favourable reviews from varied assessors, sadly the SAH-1 has not yet been a commercial success and only a handful of examples have been built.

# One

# Pioneers

The prominent British aviator Gustav Hamel visited Penzance during mid-September 1913, calling at St Michael's Mount, where he met Lord and Lady St Levan, and also at Trengwainton, home of the prominent Bolitho family. Despite variable weather, during his trip Hamel performed several exhibition flights, passed over St Ives and went on to be the first man to fly to the Land's End. As chocks were not in use at that time, his Blériot is restrained by helpers while preparations are made to start the Gnome rotary engine. *(Royal Institution of Cornwall)*

The first flights from Cornish soil were made at Penzance on 23 July 1910 by the pioneer airman Claude Grahame-White, who brought his Farman down to Penwith by train. The aircraft is shown over the British Fleets moored in Mount's Bay, with St Michael's Mount to the left. The photograph was taken from Newlyn, and may be a fake with the aircraft superimposed, but seems reasonably representative of how the event would have appeared. During his stay, Grahame-White flew his Farman from a field belonging to Poniou Farm, just east of Penzance. (*Royal Institution of Cornwall*)

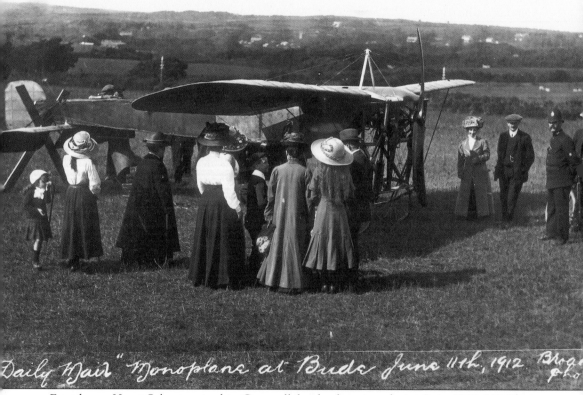

*Daily Mail" monoplane at Bude June 11th, 1912 Brog.
ph*

Frenchman Henri Salmet arrived in Cornwall for the first time during June 1912. His Blériot monoplane is seen near Bude, as admirers, mostly women, cluster round. Salmet is standing to the left of the policeman. The aircraft has its tail supported by a trestle. During this visit, Salmet called firstly at Bude, Lawhitton, Bodmin and Newquay. (*Royal Institution of Cornwall*)

Henri Salmet stands in the cockpit of his Blériot to address a crowd of interested admirers outside Truro during his June 1912 visit. His flying helmet rests on the upper fuselage decking. Later during the trip, he called at Falmouth, where he landed near the local hospital, followed by Fowey, Landrake and Liskeard. *(Royal Institution of Cornwall)*

A souvenir postcard commemorating the flying visit of Henri Salmet to Liskeard and signed by him. The date is 20 June 1912 and, in his hand-written dedication, Salmet has spelt the name of the town 'Liskard'. In fact he had just flown his flimsy Blériot in truly foul weather from Fowey to Landrake where, exhausted by his ordeal he had landed in a field and promptly fallen asleep by the aircraft, so perhaps we should forgive him! Salmet went on to give two demonstrations of flying at Liskeard during the early evening of 20 June before leaving Cornwall the following day. *(John Rapson)*

Major and Mrs Bolitho with Gustav Hamel's single-seat Blériot on 24 September 1913, as a photograph is taken in the grounds of a damp Trengwainton in commemoration of the airman's visit. Mrs Bolitho stands in a rather stylised pose while her husband sits in the cockpit. Various worthies look on, while the two policemen somewhat sheepishly join in the proceedings. (*Reg Watkiss*)

When Henri Salmet returned to tour Cornwall in April 1914 his calls included Falmouth but, in landing on Gyllyngvase Beach, he failed to take into account the soft sand there and nosed his Blériot over. Fortunately, neither Salmet nor his passenger were hurt in the accident and the aircraft was easily repaired. His tour of the south-west was promoted by the *Daily Mail* newspaper and a title to that effect was painted on the lower wing surface of the Blériot. With ironic humour, Salmet has signed the photograph, 'Bon Souvenir'. (*RCPS Research Project*)

Henri Salmet (directly below the engine cowling of his Blériot) poses with Falmouth's great and good on Gyllyngvase Beach, 27 April 1914. The aircraft has been altered to floatplane configuration. The Lady Mayoress, Mrs Chard, stands to Salmet's right; she later accompanied him on a flight that ended in engine failure off St Keverne, but the pair were towed into Mount's Bay by the tug *Marion*, where the aircraft was safely beached. *(RCPS Research Project)*

April 1914: Salmet's errant Blériot sits in the safety of the harbour at Penzance after the failure of its Gnome rotary engine while carrying Mrs Chard, revealing its clumpish float arrangement. Just visible on the fin is a crossed union Jack and Tricolour, around which was added the legend 'Entente Cordiale'. *(Royal Institution of Cornwall)*

Lord John Carbery travelled to Redruth during June 1914 where he performed exhibition flights from a farm at Sinns Barton using an 80 hp Morane two-seat monoplane numbered 12. The weather over the period was patchy, which unfortunately limited the amount of flying he was able to carry out. However, Carbery managed to give flights to a number of local people and passed over Portreath, Illogan, Chacewater, St Day, Carnmarth and Redruth itself during his stay, before returning east. A rather bedraggled tent has been erected to provide accommodation, and two of the local well-to-do look on. *(Paddy Bradley)*

Lord Carbery's smartly turned out Morane sits in the field at Sinns Barton during a period of fine weather in June 1914. The circular symbols outboard of the numerals on the lower wing surfaces were not an early attempt at military markings but were intended to help indicate the attitude of the aircraft to those watching from the ground, when manoeuvres such as the loop were demonstrated. *(Paddy Bradley)*

# Two

# The First World War

Royal Naval Air Station Mullion, summer 1917. The base was positioned near the village of Cury on land abutting the Bonython Plantations. Its vast main airship shed is in the centre of the photograph while the second shed, erected over mid-1917, is to the right – both sheds face into the prevailing south-west wind. At their entrances, huge screens have been erected to protect the airships from high winds while passing through the doors. Four aircraft, Sopwith 1 $\frac{1}{2}$ Strutters, can be seen near the single Bessoneau hangar to the lower left of the main shed. The station's accommodation, cook-house and YMCA hut are visible in the top left of the photograph while the gas and electricity generating plant is situated by the main road running parallel to the sheds. (*RCPS Research Project*)

Coastal Class airship C.9 at Mullion during the summer of 1916. Both its engines are stopped, following a return from patrol, and a large handling party manoeuvres the airship toward the safety of its shed. National markings are worn on the flight control surfaces. The windbreak at the shed entrance is under construction. In the background is a second Coastal Class. The Coastals had a crew of five or six and were capable of astonishing endurance on patrol: twenty hours was not unknown. (*J.M. Bruce/G.S. Leslie Collection*)

July 1916: Coastal C.9 prepares to embark on patrol. In the forward cockpit, wearing his flying helmet, is Flight Lieutenant J.G. Struthers, a very tenacious skipper who, unaided by surface vessels, succeeded in sinking a U-boat with bombs while flying C.9 on 21 September 1917. Struthers also participated in the probable destruction of at least three further submarines. Visible in the foreground are the handling guy ropes used by the ground crew to manoeuvre the airship. (*RNAS Culdrose*)

Looking in to the mouth of Mullion's main shed, 1918. Room was made for accommodation of two fully-inflated airships. The airships shown, C.2 and C.9, have been tethered down. Repairs and maintenance to engines, airframes and gas envelopes were carried out on site at Mullion, and the sheds housed fully-equipped engineering shops. The hydrogen gas used to inflate the envelopes was run in via underground pipes from the gas plant situated to the north-west of the shed. (*Courtesy of RNAS Culdrose*)

Proto breathing apparatus was introduced for use by the rigging crews at Mullion when working on maintenance tasks inside the airships' envelopes. Hydrogen is not poisonous, but can suffocate and the riggers worked in teams rather than alone in case of accidents.(*Courtesy of RNAS Culdrose*)

Mullion also operated single-engined Rolls-Royce Hawk-powered SSZ Class airships, which were smaller than the Coastals and had a crew of three. This example, SSZ.42, flying Naval pennants, is manoeuvring at the northern end of the station during the summer of 1918. In the background can be seen some of Mullion's hutted domestic accommodation. (*Helston Folk Musuem*)

Coastal Star Class airship C*10 operated from RNAS Mullion between July and November 1918. Only ten of these airships were built as they were viewed as an interim measure for a further (North Sea) class, the appearance of which was in fact delayed through technical difficulties. C*10 is approaching the sheds at Mullion and a windbreak is just visible. In the background are Bessoneaux hangars used to accommodate the aircraft that operated from the station. (*J.M. Bruce/G.S. Leslie Collection*).

In the larger shed at Mullion, the car of SSE.2, designed and built on site, takes shape during early 1918. Visible are the twin Rolls-Royce Hawk pusher-engined configuration, the crew's wickerwork seating arrangements and the skid undercarriage. The airship initially bore the unofficial designation M-T-1 (Mullion Twin 1) and first flew on 4 March 1918. (*RNAS Culdrose*)

Cornwall's own airship during the spring of 1918. By this time her official nomenclature had been applied to the gas envelope, along with national markings. The onlookers are civilians, which suggests SSE.2 is not on station but has descended near a village or town for some purpose. In the cockpit, the skipper, his arm gesticulating, appears to be giving instructions. Guy ropes are stowed on the airship's undercarriage supports. (*J.M Bruce/G.S. Leslie Collection*)

Over the summer of 1918, SSZ.42 visited Mullion's outstation located at Bude. Here, a small handling party is holding the guy ropes while in the background are some of the trees that afforded a degree of protection from the wind. Bude was not well-equipped with facilities, its officers being billeted nearby and the ratings living on site in bell tents. The station was located two miles south of Marhamchurch, and south east of Langford Woods. *(Ian Stratford Collection)*

Short 184 8025 arrived for service at RNAS Newlyn/Land's End in February 1917. During the following June, the aircraft was reported sinking off the Longships but was assisted by a passing drifter. Subsequently salved, it was withdrawn from use later that month as beyond repair. Here 8025 is seen accomodated at Newlyn shortly before its demise. *(Mrs Vivienne Jenkins, via Frank Marshall.)*

The construction of RNAS Tresco's large hangar commenced during the summer of 1917. After completion of its main structure, the hangar was covered with asbestos sheets. Behind the steel erecting work the engineering workshops are visible. An H.12 flying boat can be distinguished aboard its beaching trolley on the hard standing, minus its outer wings, its identity unfortunately not known. In the foreground are personnel from the RNAS Air Construction Corps. The photograph was taken roughly from the south-east. (*Mrs Vivienne Jenkins, via Frank Marshall.*)

Another view of the steelwork during the construction of RNAS Tresco's main hangar. Several figures are climbing on the structure without any visible safety arrangements. Behind the skeletal framework can be seen the power station, distinguished by its chimney. Beyond this was the domestic accommodation which started life as a collection of bell-tents. The tents were found susceptible to the strong local winds and were replaced by wooden huts. The slipway for the flying-boats is just to the right of the photograph. (*Mrs Vivienne Jenkins, via Frank Marshall.*)

RNAS Newlyn/Land's End seen from the air during the first half of 1917. The photograph was almost certainly taken from a Short 184 seaplane based on station. Newlyn/Land's End was situated on the western side of Mount's Bay, just south of Newlyn's South Pier. Initially two Bessoneau hangars were provided to accommodate the aircraft (mostly Short 184s) but later a third was added, followed by a larger and more substantial hangar. (*J.M Bruce/G.S. Leslie Collection*)

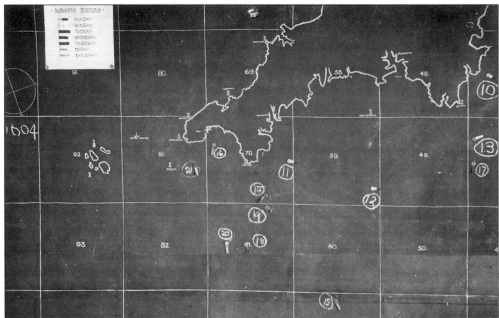

A chart used by the intelligence office at RNAS Newlyn/Land's End to mark information gathered each week on identified U-boat movements around the Cornish coastline, showing the area's lighthouses and employing a circular compass marker. The number 1604 to the left of the photograph may refer to Short 184 N1604, which struck at a German submarine in the vicinity shown, on 3 December 1917. (*J.M Bruce/G.S. Leslie Collection*)

Curtiss H.12 8654 led an eventful life after arriving at Tresco during February 1917. She was attacked by a U-boat in April and became lost in fog that June, landing up-country at Trevose Head, near Padstow. She was returned to Tresco on tow but during the journey she sustained damage to her port wings and tail. The aircraft is seen here beached at Tresco shortly after her return to the station. Her damaged wingtips, out of shot, have been removed. What appears to be the vestiges of the tow-rope are visible, while the cockpit area and propeller blades wear covers. (*Mrs Vivienne Jenkins, via Frank Marshall*)

Viewed from the mouth of a Bessoneau hangar, are three Short 184 floatplanes caught on the hard standing, two of which are undergoing maintenance, at RNAS Penzance/Newlyn in June 1917. The Newlyn Shorts later formed 424 and 425 Flights RNAS and, by August 1918, these had become 235 Squadron RAF. To the right is the tail fin of N1146, which was withdrawn from service on 1 March 1918. The other example are anonymous, the central aircraft equipped with a bomb beneath the fuselage. (*Mrs Vivienne Jenkins, via Frank Marshall*)

Curtiss H.12 8654 on the water off Tresco following repairs after her return from Trevose Head. During July 1917 she was struck at Tresco by her sister aircraft 8686, while the latter aircraft was taking off. However, she survived that episode to put in another year's service at the station before finally being stuck off. (*Mrs Vivienne Jenkins, via Frank Marshall*)

A very battered DH6, probably C7645 '23' of 236 Squadron based at Mullion, following a crash during the autumn of 1918. The aircraft has been recovered from the scene of its demise and loaded aboard a small pontoon marked PAC.17, where it sits on a makeshift wooden platform. Its wings have been removed and sit forlornly ahead of the fuselage, while naval personnel pose with their prize. (*RCPS Research Project*)

An aerial view of RNAS Padstow/Crugmeer taken from the east during the summer of 1918, showing the general configuration of the base. The four Bessoneaux aircraft hangars are prominent and in front of them are parked DH.6s. Toward the foreground is a farm house that abutted the site. Just visible behind the farmhouse are the bell tents that formed the accommodation for the majority serving at Padstow. (*Malcolm McCarthy*)

RNAS Padstow/Crugmeer in close-up from the north west, showing the bell tent accommodation and hangars. The main entrance to the station is at the junction to the left, while in the background are farm buildings. Beyond the hangars sit two DH.6s. The photograph was taken from a DH.6, the port lower wing and interconnecting strut of which is visible to the right. (*Malcolm McCarthy*)

RNAS Tresco under construction. The buildings are, from the left, the station's workshops, the main hangar, on which work has just started, the power station and the domestic area. The slipway ran approximately NNW-ESE. The moored flying-boat appears to be a Curtiss H.12, while two flying-boat hulls are apparent, one on the hard standing between the workshops and the hangar, the other on the waterline. (*J.M Bruce/G.S. Leslie Collection*)

Felixstowe F.3 N4243 arrived for service at Tresco in June 1918, joining 350/353 Flights which, in August of that year, became 234 Squadron. The aircraft is seen on the station's hard standing between the main hangar and the engineering workshops, mounted on its beaching chassis and facing the slipway. (*Mrs Vivienne Jenkins, via Frank Marshall*)

# *Three*

# Inter-war Flying

Following the end of the First World War, the RAF returned to Cornwall when the Seaplane Development Flight arrived in August 1922. Its purpose was to gain experience of operating flying-boats away from their usual coastal stations, using support ships instead. Four flying-boats participated, including Felixstowe F.5 N4839 powered by Napier Lion engines, which is seen here off the Isles of Scilly with an RAF floating dock in attendance, from the mast of which a windsock was sometimes run up. *(Frank Gibson)*

Surrey Flying Services was formed at Croydon in 1922 and provided joy-rides to thousands as the company's aircraft travelled round the country, during that decade and into the 1930s. Here, Avro 504K G-EBHM is seen 'on tour' in a field outside Truro during the summer of 1924. In the background is a support vehicle that would have contained aircraft spares, tents and rations for the staff, as well as hoardings and signs advertising the events. *(Royal Institution of Cornwall)*

Bright red Cornwall Aviation Company Avro 504K G-EBIZ and its owner, Captain Percival Phillips, (known to one and all as PP) photographed at Newquay during the summer of 1924. 'BIZ was purchased from a similar concern, the Berkshire Aviation Company, and served with Phillips between May 1924 and March 1933. It was ideal for joy-riding work, being cheap to buy, easy to maintain and rugged, while its low take-off and landing speeds made it suitable for operation from the impromptu airstrips (often farmers' fields) usually employed by the company. *(Author's Collection)*

Test-flying Avro 504K G-EBIZ at St Austell during the mid-1920s. Percival Phillips is at the controls. The Cornish Aviation Company used a number of landing fields around St Austell for their activities, according to availability and the priorities of the landowners concerned. The field at nearby Rocky Parc was sometimes employed for agricultural shows, so an alternative landing strip was made available at Venton Wyn, on the north side of the main St Austell-Truro road. (*Dave Phillips*)

During September 1925, PP and G-EBIZ travelled to Paignton. From left to right: Mike Crocker, F.E. Gerry Draycott, PP, and Mr and Mrs A.J. Adams. Adams, a licensed engineer, was a versatile man, who became the company's Commercial Manager and also participated in the wing-walking shows. Draycott too was an engineer. The aircraft was affectionately known, within the Phillips family, as *Geebies*. (*Author's Collection*)

Cornwall Aviation's Avro 504K G-EBIZ ready for duty. The aircraft is surrounded by the paraphernalia used by the company. In the background over the gate into the field is a sign (though this seems to be advertising BP spirit rather than the event itself), and the lorry carrying spares, provisions, tents, tickets and the windsock is parked nearby. The wife of A.J. Adams sits side-saddle on PP's motorcycle, while his deckchair is placed in a sunny spot by the lorry. Standing by the engine cowling of 'BIZ is Adams. (*Author's Collection*)

Percival Phillips about to commence a test flight in *Geebies* from a field at Venton Wyn during 1930. The passengers are both engineers. Just discernible in the background beyond the rear fuselage is one of St Austell's famous 'white mountains' – a waste heap from the local China Clay industry. (*Author's Collection*)

April 1928 found the Cornwall Aviation Company at Eltham, where the Mayor of Woolwich, Councillor G.H. Langham, pale but determined, posed for his photograph at the top of the boarding ladder while preparing himself for his coming flight in G-EBIZ. His town clerk, Sir Arthur Bryceson, standing, accompanied the Mayor. PP is in the cockpit, while in the background is a banner advertising the day's event. (*Author's Collection*)

In 1929 a landplane finally travelled to the Isles of Scilly. On 19 August a de Havilland DH.60G Gypsy Moth (probably G-AAKI or G-AAKU), piloted by Colonel the Master of (later Lord) Semphill, landed on the golf course near Carn Morval, on the north-west side of the island, after a flight from a field on the Lizard. The local population seems fascinated by the apparition and a couple of individuals appear to be leaning on it. (*Reg Watkiss*)

On 10 October 1930 another caller came to the Isles of Scilly, but that time to Tresco: Wright-Bellanca WB.2 NR237 *Columbia*, flown by Capt Errol Boyd with Lt Harry Connor. The two had planned a non-stop journey from Newfoundland to Croydon but the rear fuel tank feed developed a fault so, prudently, a landing was made on Pentle Beach, to the eastern side of Tresco, during the early evening. The following day the fuel system was corrected and the Bellanca took off from the beach to complete its journey. (*Author's Collection*)

Cornwall Aviation Company's Avro 504K G-EBSE seen at Sticker during the 1930 season. The airstrip was situated some two miles along the Truro road from St Austell. Altogether the company used seven Avro 504Ks: G-EBIZ, G-EBNR, G-EBSE, G-AAAF, G-AAYI, G-ABHI and G-AAUJ. BSE served between July 1927 and April 1932. (*Mrs J. Church*)

Aviation Tours Ltd was a barn-storming concern similar to the Cornwall Aviation Company and also toured the country extensively. On 16 August 1932 the show came to Wadebridge, where interspersing the usual joy-riding for the public, Martin Hearn gave his truly formidable and nerveless display of wing-walking – not for the faint-hearted! Hearn has autographed and dated this souvenir photograph. (RCPS *Research Project*)

Padstow witnessed an unusual visitation when Supermarine Southampton S1232/2 of 204 Squadron developed engine trouble off north Cornwall during May 1931. F/O F R Worthington put S1232 down in the sea some fifteen miles north of Trevose Head with a defective starboard Napier Lion Va. The steamer Skeloon towed the Southampton into Padstow harbour as seen here, where repairs were duly effected. The aircraft was then able to make a safe return to its station at RAF Mount Batten. The crew clusters round the offending engine; the other has been covered over. (*Malcolm McCarthy*)

Alan Cobham's National Aviation Day Displays circus travelled to Cornwall several times during the 1930s. Here, joy-riding Airspeed Ferry G-ABSJ is seen at Porthmissen Farm, Padstow, on 2 September 1933, as local people have a souvenir photograph taken. The Ferry was specially commissioned for Cobham, who required good short-field performance combined with plentiful passenger-carrying capability: the Ferry seated ten. *(Malcolm McCarthy)*

During the Cobham exhibition at Padstow on 2 September 1933, the public was treated to a demonstration of parachuting made from Tiger Moth G-ACEZ by Mr W. Harris. The parachutist makes ready to go aloft, while the pilot observes his preparations from the rear seat of the aircraft. The jumps were made from an altitude of around 2,000ft. *(Malcolm McCarthy)*

On 6 August 1934 Alan Cobham's circus came to Falmouth, where the aircraft flew from Boskensoe Farm just outside the town. The types present on that occasion once again included Tiger Moth G-ACEZ. This aircraft was sometimes flown by Flt Lt Geoffrey Tyson, who was able to pick up handkerchiefs from the ground using hooks attached to the wingtips – some exhibition of precision flying! (*RCPS Research Project*)

Supermarine Southampton IIs from 204 Squadron were based at RAF Mount Batten at Plymouth between February 1929 and September 1935. During their stay, examples used occasionally to visit Cornish harbours, notably Falmouth, where this early example, S1044/1, is seen. Note the large wireless aerial above the upper wing. (*RCPS Research Project*)

DH84 Dragon G-ACKD *Saturn* was used by Provincial Airways on the first Cornish commercial air route, which opened during April 1934, linking Plymouth with Hayle. By August, Provincial's service included another Cornish stop at Newquay but, unfortunately, the company went into liquidation in September 1935. (*Peter H.T. Green*)

The Jubilee Air Display travelled to Racecourse Farm, near Bodmin, on 16 August 1935. Tragically, during the course of the day Jubilee Air Displays' yellow Avro 504N G-ADBS (ex-K1251) crashed at nearby Lancarffe Farm, diving into a field almost opposite the land on which the display was based. The three people aboard the aircraft died; they were George Anderson the pilot, mechanic Ronald Jope, and Arthur Lyne, son of the Mayor of Bodmin, Alderman Browning Lyne. The loss of 'DBS was the worst air crash in Cornwall up to that time. (*Peter H.T. Green*)

During the autumn of 1936, five Short Singapore III flying-boats of 209 Squadron based at Felixstowe made the trip to Falmouth, in order to investigate the potential of the harbour there to provide facilities suitable for their operation. This impressive presence drew large crowds from the town. Whatever the assessment made, however, the Singapores did not return. (*RCPS Research Project*)

On 15 September 1937 the first scheduled service opened between Land's End and St Mary's, the operator being Channel Air Ferries. The aircraft in use was DH.84 Dragon G-ADCR. Four passengers flew to St Mary's, departing from St Just at 9 a.m. and arriving twenty minutes later, while five passengers made the return flight. While a small boy admires the aircraft, a passenger lights up a cigarette – was he a nervous traveller? Today the journey is not much quicker but the route vastly more subscribed, especially in the summer season. (*Royal Institution of Cornwall*)

Channel Air Ferries Dragon, probably G-ADCR, at St Just with a visiting van from beyond the Tamar. To the right is New Zealander Captain Dustin, a Provincial pilot, who tragically lost his life when the Dragon crashed in fog at St Just on Saturday 25 June 1938. *(Mike Ingham)*

Channel Air Ferries' second Dragon was G-ACPY, which had previously been registered in Ireland to Aer Lingus as EI-ABI *Iolar* and was the first aircraft operated by that carrier. 'CPY came to the company via the Olley Air Service concern and served with Channel between March 1938 and March 1939; it is seen at St Just during that period. A woman stands in the slipstream of the port engine, next to the wheeled steps placed by the cabin door – her hat must be very well pinned on! *(Frank Gibson)*

Western Airways' DH.86B G-AETM joined the company in 1939 and that season flew the route between Swansea, Barnstaple, Newquay and Penzance. This aircraft was formerly used by Allied Airways and named *Silver Star*. At Newquay, the company flew from Trebelzue Big Field, previously occupied by Alan Cobham's displays and destined to become an RAF station. *(Author's Collection)*

Channel Air Ferries also operated de Havilland DH.83 Fox Moth G-ACFF from St Just. The aircraft arrived in Cornwall during the spring of 1939 and over the summer was used to provide joy-rides for well-heeled tourists. It was finally impressed for military duty as X9305 during April 1940. The aircraft did not have to travel far to carry out its war work, being employed by A Flight, No.1 Anti Aircraft Co-operation Unit at Cleave and Western Zoyland. To the right of the photograph are two (probably the only two) buses used to carry passengers to and from the airfield. *(Mike Ingham)*

Saunders-Roe London II K5260 VQ-U, operated by 201 Squadron, was based at Calshot but over the summer of 1939 visited the River Fal, as seen here. The object of the call was to reassess the suitability of the area for flying-boat operations should the need arise. The London was equipped with an overload fuel tank positioned on the upper fuselage decking behind the cockpit. The Squadron badge, a seagull, wings elevated, is painted within a six-pointed star on the nose of the aircraft. K5260 was eventually lost off Gibraltar during August 1940. During the war, the Fal saw only occasional visits from flying-boats. (*RCPS Research Project*)

Some Blackburn Skua dive-bombers found alternative employment as target tugs, numbers joining No.2 Anti Aircraft Co-operation Unit. This example is seen at Cleave's No.6 Heavy Anti Aircraft Practice Camp shortly before the outbreak of war, at which time it wore no camouflage. The aircraft stands tall, consistent with the carrier-borne landings for which it was designed. The admirers are from Cleave artillery camp, though one is sporting what appears to be a naval cap. (*Tim Bishop*)

# Four

# The Second World War

The de Havilland DH.82B Queen Bee radio-controlled target aircraft was based around the Tiger Moth and provided the climax of many of Cleave's anti-aircraft gunnery courses. Despite their hazardous employment, several examples achieved a longevity surprising not only in view of their role, but also considering the difficulties in landing them successfully following the exercises. Here, a Queen Bee of V Flight, No.1 AACU is seen with engine running, being prepared for take-off on the Cleave steam catapult during 1940. *(Bill Young via Tim Bishop)*

A chocked line-up of four Westland Wallace target tugs at Cleave during 1940, property of G Flight, No.1 AACU. The aircraft are parked by one of the Bessoneaux hangars on the southern part of the airfield. The target winch windmill apparatus is visible just aft of the rear cockpit of the nearest example. The tugs also serviced nearby No.10 Light Anti Aircraft Practice Camp at St Agnes Head and No.12 LAAPC at Penhale. (*Bill Young*)

Cleave airfield and No.6 Heavy Anti Aircraft Practice Camp in early 1940. The trainee gunners' accommodation and the camp's facilities are to the left, much of it consisting of wooden huts, marquees and bell tents. The hangars and grass taxiways are to the centre while to the right is the grass area used to provide runways. At that time, three composite First World War vintage Bessoneaux hangars were employed at Cleave. Just visible by the hangars are two Wallace target tugs. Later, the steam catapult was installed in order to launch the station's Queen Bee pilotless floatplanes. Across the grass area are signs of the Cornish hedges that have been removed to make way for the flying. (*Bill Young*)

Hawker Henley target tug L3426 of G Flight, No.1 AACU following its demise at Cleave on 28 March 1940. The aircraft swung on take-off, hit a tree and crash-landed on a steep slope near the station. The Henley was extensively damaged. Just visible in the background is the sea. (*Bill Young via Tim Bishop*)

On 21 August 1940, three Junkers Ju 88 bombers made a low-level attack against St Eval. The No.4 Hangar, occupied by 236 Squadron, was severely damaged and No.3 Hangar was also hit. Thirty casualties were suffered, while three of the Blenheim fighters inside were destroyed and others damaged. No.238 Squadron Hurricanes were hurriedly scrambled, intercepting the departing bombers and shooting down two. The car in the foreground gives scale to the battered hangar. (*Gerry Holder*)

On 25 August 1940 Pilot Officer Leonard Joseph Dejace is seen standing beneath the nose of a 236 Squadron Blenheim IVF fighter at St Eval. One of several Belgian pilots with the Squadron at that time, he was known as Paul. In the far distance are two Coastal Command Ansons and one of the station's C Type hangars. *(Gerry Holder)*

Over the autumn of 1940, No.247 Squadron's Gloster Gladiators were flown in each evening from Roborough (Plymouth) to St Eval in an attempt to provide some night fighting strength against incoming bombers. Roborough did not lend itself to night flying, hence the need to base the Squadron at two stations. No.247 came under St Eval's control and went operational at Roborough during mid-August. Generally, six aircraft flew from Roborough during the day while three (later four and finally, six) were made available at St Eval during each night. Here, N2308 HP-B sits in the Devonshire sunshine before embarking to Cornwall for night duty. *(247 Squadron Association)*

No.247 Squadron had exchanged their Gladiators for Hurricane Is by February 1941. HP-A (possibly W9153) is seen at rest near St Eval's perimeter track during the following spring. Fitters are carrying out engine maintenance and the aircraft's cowlings have been removed. To the left is parked a second Hurricane and to the right a photographic reconnaissance Spitfire. *(247 Squadron Association)*

No.247 Squadron moved to Predannack during their stay in Cornwall, arriving in June 1941. Here, ground crew pose with two of the Squadron's cannon-armed black Hurricane IICs, giving the impression for the Public Relations photographer that maintenance is being carried out, although no equipment or tools are visible. The aircraft are fitted with small shields at the upper rear area of the engine cowling in order to protect the pilot's night vision from the glare of the exhausts during nocturnal missions. *(RNAS Culdrose)*

The ground crew of 66 Squadron Spitfire IIA LZ-R pose with their charge at Perranporth during 1941. This aircraft was the personal mount of 'Laddie' Lucas, who pre-war had gained renown as a Walker Cup golfer and who rose to the rank of Wing Commander. No.66 Squadron stayed at Perranporth until December 1941 when a move took place to nearby Portreath. *(via Bob Andrew)*

The nomadic Westland Whirlwind I twin-engined fighters of 263 Squadron served at St Eval and Portreath during 1941. This is P6969 HE-V, sporting a rather battered camouflage scheme, which was lost off Dodman Point on 8 February 1941 during an action in which an Arado Ar 196 was also destroyed. *(Imperial War Museum)*

In June 1941, No.130 Squadron arrived at Portreath with their Spitfire IIAs. Squadron members congregate in front of Spitfire IIA PJ-V, which sports a natty line in spinner décor and mounts an overload fuel tank beneath the port wing. The scene is photographed in an aircraft blast protection pen. (*G. Perry Bauchman*)

St Eval's 217 Squadron traded in their Avro Ansons over a lengthy period, finally going operational with the Bristol Beaufort during December 1940 though the first three examples, all dual-control Mk Is, had arrived with the unit for conversion training during the previous May. Seen here is L9878 MW-R, which was eventually struck off charge in May 1943. (*Author's collection*)

As air attacks began from Britain against occupied Europe, Blenheim light bombers of No.2 Group Bomber Command started to appear in Cornwall. This is RT-W of 114 Squadron which made a visit to the grass of Cleave during the latter half of 1941, an unscheduled one for the north Cornish station was usually concerned only with target towing and drone aircraft, while 114 were never stationed in the county. No.114 Squadron transferred from West Raynham to Algeria in November 1942. *(Bill Young)*

A St Eval Beaufort, from 217 Squadron, visited Fowey on 21 April 1941 during the town's War Weapons Week. The aircraft is seen performing before local people at Squire's Field. Over the course of the week, a magnificent £41,412 was raised toward the war effort. During the war, aircraft were used to promote such savings activities across Britain and often combined their public duties with air tests and training sorties. *(Paul Richards)*

No.206 Squadron operated Hudson Is from St Eval on anti-submarine and shipping reconnaissance missions during the early summer of 1941. This example is P5143 VX-F: it went on to serve with No.1 Operational Training Unit and later the Air Transport Auxiliary before being struck off charge in April 1945. Over twenty squadrons of the RAF were equipped with the Hudson during the Second World War. No.206 later flew to Fortresses from Davidstow in 1942 and, during the spring of 1944, converted to Liberators when the squadron returned briefly to St Eval. (*Author's collection*).

Members of 130 Squadron stand beside a line-up of their Spitfire VAs and VBs during early 1942. By that time of this photograph the Squadron had left Portreath and was flying from nearby Perranporth. The unit took part in convoy patrols and sweeps over northern France as well as contributing to the air cover over Cornwall and Devon. (*Denys Bryant*)

This vertical of Trebelzue, near Newquay, was taken on 5 April 1942, by which time the station had already been condemned as inadequate for the major aircraft ferrying task ahead and the need to construct a larger replacement airfield nearby had been recognized. Trebelzue became an aircraft parking area subsumed by St Mawgan when that airfield went operational in August 1943. (*Peter H.T. Green*)

Armstrong Whitworth Whitley VII BD681/N of No.10 Operational Training Unit forms the background to a group photograph of F/O Phillips and his crew in June 1943 during the time the unit was detached to St Eval. No.10 OTU was employed in anti-submarine and shipping patrols and suffered dreadful crew losses during its time in Cornwall. On 12 July 1943, BD681 was shot down by a Ju 88 over the Bay of Biscay. (*Peter H.T. Green*).

Despite the drastic reduction in commercial aviation following the outbreak of the Second World War, the Great Western & Southern Air Lines Land's End-St Mary's route was considered important and continued almost constantly throughout the war years, using camouflaged DH.89 Dragon Rapides as seen here. Second from the right is Captain Morris Hearn, who went on to fly the route almost until the DH.89s were replaced by Sea King helicopters. *(Mrs J. Church)*

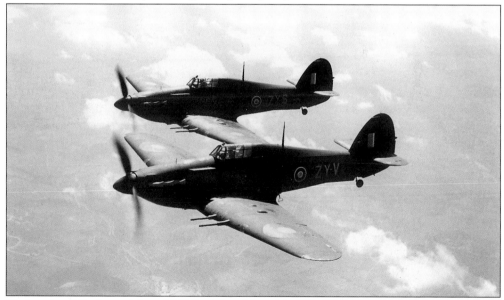

Black-painted Predannack-based 247 Squadron Hurricane IICs BE634 ZY-V (Commanding Officer, Canadian Sqn Ldr Pete O'Brian) and BD936 ZY-S (Sous-Lt Helies) in close formation over Cornwall during April 1942. This foray was carried out for the benefit of the public relations photographer, who was flown that day in a Douglas Havoc, probably from 1457 Flight which was also based at Predannack. *(RNAS Culdrose)*

The moment of truth as a DH.82B Queen Bee floatplane is launched from the Cleave catapult. The aircraft makes an odd spectacle in that it is (of course) bereft of any crew. The catapult was situated at the cliff edge facing out to sea, and its concrete plinth is still *in situ* today. The Queen Bee was very slow compared with the enemy aircraft that the trainee gunners at Cleave might eventually face but nonetheless provided a realism lacking in a simple towed target. *(Bill Young)*

Ouch! A Cleave Queen Bee landplane target aircraft in reduced circumstances on the clifftop near the airfield. The identity of the aircraft appears to be N1826; it does not seem to have been hit by artillery fire so presumably it has crashed either due to operator error or equipment malfunction, probably the former. Damage appears to be confined to undercarriage, engine cowling and propeller. Despite such accidents, some of Cleave's Queen Bees achieved a remarkably long lifespan. N1826 was eventually shot down at the Anglesey ranges during June 1941. *(Bill Young)*

During the afternoon of 15 May 1943, a rare visitor called at Fowey in the form of a Coastal Command Catalina, which moored off Town Quay there. The aircraft was sent to inspire the residents of the Fowey and Polruan areas who were hoping to raise the sum of £20,000, enough to purchase an entire Catalina, through their Wings for Victory week held that month. In fact, an enormous £43,152 was presented at the end of the event. In the background, the buildings by the river bank have received camouflage paintwork. *(Paul Richards)*

Seafire IIC MB319, seen at St Merryn during 1943. The Naval trainee ground crew smother the aircraft while posing energetically for the benefit of the camera. One exercise not possible for the trainees to carry out with the Seafire IIC was wing-folding drill, for not until the introduction of the later Seafire III was such a wing introduced. *(Author's collection)*

Weathered Swordfish P4017 S6-C of 774 Squadron Fleet Air Arm at St Merryn helps out with an exercise during a training session over the summer of 1943. The trainees wield a trolley, but only a glimpse of its load is visible through the massed legs of the personnel: it appears to be either a bomb or a torpedo. (*Author's collection*)

The smaller of St Merryn's watch towers, 1943. Many of the station's buildings survive in remarkably intact condition even today, including the tower. Some are still in use, notably by gyrocopter enthusiasts and by the Cornwall Parachute Centre; the station is well worth a visit. (*Author's collection*)

USAAF C-87A Liberator 439206, seen parked in front of St Mawgan's tower during 1944. In the distance to the right are parked a total of eighteen Dakotas of which several are visible here. (*Via R.C.B. Ashworth*)

Wellington XIV of 304 (*Slaski*) Squadron at Davidstow Moor during mid-September 1943. The aircraft is possibly HF188 2-A; the Squadron was manned by Polish personnel. In the background is a Wellington X or XIII, also operated by the Squadron at that time. Behind the background aircraft is the hill known as Bray Down, situated south-west of the airfield. (*Rod Knight*)

Beaufighter TF10 NE355 2-H of 404 Squadron Royal Canadian Air Force at rest at RAF Davidstow Moor during the spring of 1944. It carries rocket projectiles, which were used with devastating effect to strike at enemy ground forces and shipping. No.404's posting to Davidstow was brief, lasting between 10 May and 1 July 1944. During this time the Squadron covered the western flank of the Allied invasion of France. (*Public Archives of Canada Ref:PL41003*)

Two Spitfires of 165 Squadron sit at readiness at Predannack during the early summer of 1944. Nos165 and 1 Squadrons joined forces at Predannack between April and June 1944, forming a Spitfire Wing flying sweeps over north-west France, convoy patrols, escorts and fighter-bomber missions until both units moved, 165 to Detling on 22 June and 1 Squadron also to Detling, via Harrowbeer, on the same day. (*Imperial War Museum*)

A Coastal Command Liberator crew receiving a briefing prior to commencing a patrol from St Eval during 1944. The aircraft carries the code 'H'. The rear defensive armament is shown to advantage. These aircraft carried depth charges on anti-submarine missions over the Channel, the Western Approaches and into the Bay of Biscay. (*Author's collection*)

Fleet Air Arm rocket-equipped 816 Squadron Swordfish NF243 'S', accompanied by 'K', wearing D-Day invasion stripes. Flying from Perranporth, the Swordfish carried out round-the-clock sorties over the Channel against enemy shipping over the early summer of 1944, before moving back to RNAS St Merryn in July of that year where the Squadron promptly disbanded, its work done. (*Fred Motley via Bob Andrew*)

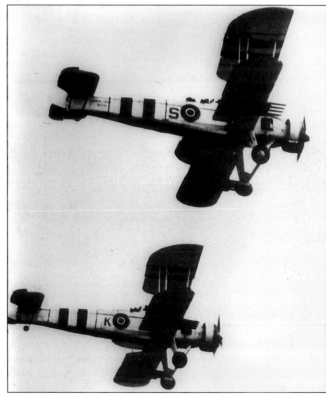

No.165 Squadron personnel line up casually on a damp day at Predannack during the early summer of 1944, together with a spaniel, in front of one of the Squadron's Spitfires. No.165 later converted to Mustangs at Bentwater, operating the American type on long-range missions from February 1945 until the war's end. (*Author's collection*)

Members of 151 Squadron with one of the unit's Mosquitos providing a backdrop during the brief posting to Predannack, July 1944. The Squadron was employed at that time in intruder patrols and anti-shipping work. The aircraft is wearing underwing D-Day invasion stripesBack: P/O Norman, Sgt Anderson, P/O Phillips, Flt Lt Handley. Front: W/O Cunningham, F/Sgt Williams. (*Laurie Cunningham*)

Ground crew at work on a St Eval Coastal Command Liberator between missions during 1944; the aircraft is coded P-2. The maintenance platforms used to reach the engines are wheeled for ease of mobility. The crew are well wrapped against the elements. In the background a second Liberator awaits its turn for attention. (*Author's collection*)

Spitfire PR XIs of 541 Squadron seen on detachment from St Eval to St Mawgan during 1944. These aircraft carried out photo-reconnaissance missions over occupied north-west Europe. At that time the Squadron's home station was Benson.(*J. Oliver via R.C.B. Ashworth*)

St Merryn's north-east dispersal viewed from 500ft on 26 August 1944. Visible are a variety of buildings including large and small hangars and a few Nissan huts. This part of the station appears tranquil amidst the Cornish countryside, with seemingly few aircraft in attendance. (*Author's collection*)

A 276 Squadron Warwick under power at Portreath during the early autumn of 1944. The aircraft wears invasion stripes, and carries an airborne lifeboat beneath its fuselage. In the background is a second Warwick. (*Ian Collett*)

St Eval, 1945: two likely lads pose with a Warwick from 179 Squadron. No.179 flew anti-submarine patrols from both Predannack (April to September 1944) and St Eval (from November 1944), remaining at the latter station after the war until September 1946 when it disbanded. *(Author's collection)*

St Mawgan viewed from the air during 1945. The station's main runway is in the foreground, where dispersal areas can also be seen. In the distance toward the coastline are the old Trebelzue facilities, employed by St Mawgan for additional room as the need arose. *(Via R.C.B. Ashworth)*

An aerial view of Davidstow Moor. Though the photograph was taken in 1984, the arrangement of Davidstow has remained unchanged since the departure of the RAF and some of the buildings there are still occupied today, notably by an enthusiastic microlight flying club. The station watch tower, long abandoned, is visible in the top left. (*Via R.C.B. Ashworth*)

At the end of the Second World War, several of the airborne lifeboats formerly carried by St Eval's Air Sea Rescue Warwicks were liberated and adapted by some enterprising souls into sailing dinghies, which were used by the St Eval Sailing Club on the River Camel at Padstow and around the local coastline. The Club took over the wartime ASR station and the adjacent bungalow at Hawkers Cove, on the western bank of the mouth of the river, which had been used by the crew of a high-speed rescue launch stationed there. (*Author's collection*)

# *Five*

# Civil Flying: 1945-1970

Great Western & Southern Air Lines' Dragon Rapide G-ACPP at St Mary's during 1945. Great Western's Land's End-Scillies service continued almost throughout hostilities. Though the war was over when this photograph was taken, the aircraft has yet to be repainted in its civil colour scheme. From right to left: Canadian newly-weds, Captain Hearne and 'CPP's radio officer. Behind the bride, drawn on the aircraft is a cartoon cat and the legend 'Who's just married?' (*Mrs J. Church*)
Dragon Rapide G-ACPP – another view of the Canadian wedding party at St Mary's. To

accommodate the entire group in one journey would have been an exceedingly tight fit and they were no doubt transported in two hops. Captain Hearne served on the Land's End-St Mary's route, continuing to fly Rapides, until March 1962. Over that time he logged 31,560 flights and some 15,000 hours and was awarded the Queen's Commendation at his retirement ceremony. *(Mrs J. Church)*

Dragon Rapide G-ACPP at St Mary's during 1946, showing its restored but short-lived Great Western & Southern Air Lines civilian livery. Its windows have been cleaned of the paint that had been applied during the war years to prevent passengers observing shipping movements. Captain Hearne is second from the left. The landing light of the aircraft has been unmasked, its former wartime cover removed. *(Mrs J. Church)*

During the summer of 1949, Plymouth and District Aero Club started to use the old Trebelzue end of St Mawgan for charter and pleasure flying. The Club's ex-Air Transport Auxiliary Fairchild Argus 2, G-AJOZ (ex-FK338), is seen at rest on the airfield's wartime runway during June of the following year. 'JOZ survived until August 1962 when it crashed at Rennes. *(Paul Longthorp)*

On 24 June 1950 the Mayor of Newquay, Mr Billingham, welcomed the inaugural tourist flight from Manchester Ringway to Cornwall by Fingland's Airways Ltd. He is seen greeting the company's Captain Prowse at the Trebelzue end of St Mawgan. Forming the backdrop is Fingland's Anson G-AKFM, ex-MG495. Fingland's operated a Cornish route until the autumn of 1952 when the company ceased flying. *(Paul Longthorp)*

Trebelzue received a visit from Dove 2 G-ALVD of Dunlop Aviation during August 1950. The Dove 2 was a six-seat executive version of the marque. 'LVD was sold to a Pakistani buyer during 1956. (*Paul Longthorp*)

Refuelling the Plymouth and District Aero Club's Argus 'JOZ at Trebelzue in the autumn sunshine during September 1950. The Club also flew a Tiger Moth and two Austers, and operated under the supervision of Wing Commander R.J. Pearce, who had previously worked for Power Jets. (*Paul Longthorp*)

*Opposite page, top*: Consul G-AIKX (ex-PK302) owned by S. Hodge and Sons called at Trebelzue during September 1950. A group poses before the aircraft in the typically blustery conditions experienced by the exposed location. The Consul was one of a small number of private aircraft that used the airfield before the Air Ministry reclaimed the airfield for its own activities in April 1951. G-AIKX was eventually scrapped at Croydon in September 1956. (*Paul Longthorp*)

For the 1951 holiday season, Murray Chown Aviation opened a route connecting Perranporth with Staverton and Guernsey using Rapide G-AIYP, which also carried out a number of charter flights that year. Seen at Perranporth with the Rapide during June 1951 are Murray Chown personnel Paul Longthorp, Ray Chown, Bob Slade, George Garland, Jerry Tonkin and Doug Phillips. At that time, all three wartime runways at Perranporth were still serviceable. *(Paul Longthorp)*

On 8 July 1951 a Mr Drake, a potato merchant by trade, flew with his wife to Perranporth in his Auster J/1 Autocrat G-AJIV. Unfortunately, the aircraft undershot the runway and hit a barbed wire boundary fence. The tailwheel caught in the wire and 'JIV dragged a line of fence-posts with it, coming to rest in a field of long grass. Happily, both pilot and passenger survived. The Auster was stored briefly at Perranporth but was subsequently written off. *(Paul Longthorp)*

Murray Chown Aviation Proctor G-AIEG and Rapide G-AIYP at Land's End during the 1951 holiday season. During that year, the company's Cornish centre of operations moved from Trebelzue to Perranporth, as the Air Ministry asserted its right to exclusive use of Trebelzue and St Mawgan. *(Paul Longthorp)*

Murray Chown used Chrislea CH.3 Super Ace 2 G-AKVD during 1951. It is seen at Perranporth over the summer of that year, by the buildings that would later be occupied by the Perranporth Gliding (and Flying) Club. In the background is a vehicle marked with the name of Murray Chown Aviation Ltd that appears once to have been an improvised armoured car! The aircraft was bought in February 1953 by Honda Motors of Yokohama, becoming JA-3062. (*Paul Longthorp*)

Murray Chown's Proctor G-AIEG with George Garland at Land's End during the summer of 1951. The company's intent in positioning the aircraft at Land's End was to tempt passengers from the conveniently passing Wallace Arnold tourist coaches into the Proctor for short pleasure flights. The coach drivers were in league with the aviators and received free flights in return for coach passengers 'safely delivered' to the airfield! Among the favourite trips were those that took in the Wolf Rock and Bishop's Rock lighthouses. (*Paul Longthorp*)

The Land's End-St Mary's service operated by BEA was one of the most popular internal flights of its time. Served by DH.89 Rapides, during the high season it was not uncommon for the aircraft to make over twenty round trips each day. DH.89A Dragon Rapide G-AHXW *John Nicholson* is spotted at St Mary's during the early 1950s. (*Author's collection*)

BEA's Rapides flew the Land's End-St Mary's route throughout the 1950s and into the following decade. G-AKZB *Lord Baden Powell* is seen at Land's End with passengers about to board. This aircraft was eventually written off in an accident while landing there in fog during December 1961. (*Author's collection*)

The wonderfully-rural setting of Land's End airfield during the late 1950s, showing the extent of the wooden buildings, including a refreshment hut, behind which is parked a motor coach used to ferry passengers to and from nearby resorts. Beyond the buildings was situated the pre-war hangar, which was big enough to accommodate two DH.89s. BEA's Dragon G-AHLL is at rest on the grass. This aircraft, named *Sir Henry Lawrence*, was involved in an accident on 21 May 1959 after it overran the runway at Land's End and struck a Cornish (stone) hedge; it was subsequently written off. (*Author's collection*)

Disembarking from BEA Rapide G-AHKU at Land's End during the 1950s. The fabric covered airframe of the aircraft, named *Cecil John Rhodes* is visible, as is the Royal Mail symbol on the tailplane. (*Royal Institution of Cornwall*)

Dakota G-AMPY of Starways seen at St Mawgan during 1963, parked at the edge of what appears to be part of a wartime blast pen. The Starways route from Liverpool to St Mawgan was inaugurated in June 1959 and the following year routes were opened from Birmingham, Glasgow, Manchester and Newcastle. 'MPY had joined Starways during March 1952 and survived in service until the company's take-over. (*Author's collection*)

Big brother to the Starways DC.3s, C.54A Skymaster G-ARIY is caught at St Mawgan in May 1963 shortly before the company stopped trading. In November of that year, Starways signed a co-operation agreement with British Eagle International Airlines and the following month ceased operations, British Eagle taking over all the former Starways routes. G-ARIY, which had entered service with Starways during February 1961, was withdrawn from use during the following year. (*Dennis Ellery*)

BEA's Rapide G-AHKU caught at speed on the runway at St Mary's during the early 1960s. This aircraft survived to form part of BEA's final fleet of three such aircraft during 1964, the other two being G-AJCL, a second *Sir Henry Lawrence* replacing G-AKZB, and G-AGSH *Lord Baden-Powell*. (*Frank Gibson*)

Sikorsky S61-N helicopters G-ASNL and G-ASNM arrived at St Mary's on 1 May 1964. On the following day, the S61-Ns took over the BEA service from the elderly DH.89s. Dignitaries invited for the inauguration of the new type are visible walking toward the helicopters. Two of the three surviving BEA Rapides, G-AJCL and G-AHKU, watch the newcomers but for them, a new owner was looming. (*Frank Gibson*)

St Merryn had lain fallow since its closure in January 1956, with only the odd visitor after that time. One of the oddest surely was this Bensen B7 gyro-glider, towed by a car along the old runways during the early 1960s by an early group of local enthusiasts. The pilot in the right-hand seat looks comfortable enough but his passenger appears far from relaxed! In the background is a wartime hangar. The early gyrocopter folk at St Merryn clashed with some local people who complained of the noise (not from the example shown, admittedly), but eventually an accommodation was reached and all now co-exist happily. *(Via Chris Julian)*

Despite its antiquity, Rapide G-AJCL found a new operator following its departure from BEA, rather than joining the unemployment scrapheap. It was purchased by British Westpoint Airlines in May 1964, serving until May 1966. 'JCL is seen being refuelled at St Mawgan during September 1965. (*R.C.B. Ashworth*)

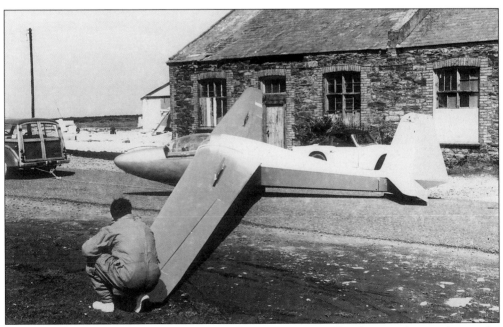

An EoN Olympia 463 glider at Perranporth during May 1966. The photograph was taken at the northern end of the airfield, among the former wartime buildings subsequently acquired by the Perranporth Gliding (and Flying) Club, which is still very much a thriving concern today. A Morris Traveller prepares to tow the aircraft to the Perranporth runway away to the south. (*R.C.B. Ashworth*)

British Eagle International Airlines Viscount 732 G-ANRS *City of Newcastle* at Newquay during July 1966. The aircraft is at rest near the tiny civil terminal originally forming Newquay Airport and situated on the greater RAF St Mawgan, which continues to be the arrangement today though the civil side has since been rebuilt and much enlarged. 'NRS stayed with the company until the concern's sudden demise in late 1968. *(R.C.B. Ashworth)*

British Midland's Dakota G-AOGZ being refuelled at Newquay during August 1966, the first year of the company's service from Castle Donington. 'OGZ was sold off later in the year as Viscounts were phased in by the company. *(R.C.B. Ashworth)*

Graceful LET L.13 Blanik glider G-ASZL at rest at the perimeter of Land's End airfield, August 1967. The aircraft belonged to the Land's End Gliding Club, along with two single-seat gliders and an Auster aero-tow. Sadly, the club closed down in 1968, many of its members joining the nearby Culdrose Gliding Club; the Blanik too migrated there. G-ASZL was one of the very few gliders to appear on the British Civil Register and became BGA 1347 before being written off during January 1970. (R.C.B. Ashworth)

Scillonia Airways' dapper Rapide G-AHGC *Tresco* seen at Land's End during August 1968. Behind is a second example, either G-AHAG *Bryher* or G-AJCL *Samson*, and in the background a third, G-AHKU *Bishop*. 'HGC is minus its port engine; a cover has been placed over the dismantled area. (R.C.B. Ashworth)

British Eagle Bristol Britannia 312 G-AOVG *Bounteous* about to land at St Mawgan during the summer of 1968. At that time the company was operating a London-Newquay route and also many of the old Starways routes that it had inherited by acquisition. 'OVG arrived for service during April 1964 and stayed until British Eagle's collapse in November of that year. *(Dennis Ellery)*

Percival Proctor V G-AGTC seen at Perranporth during 1968, by which time the aircraft was unknowingly near the end of its life: it was damaged beyond repair near Malaga during May 1969. In the background are some of the airfield's wartime RAF buildings. *(Barry Cole)*

BEA's S-61N G-AWFX force-landed at Long Rock on flooded ground abutting Penzance Heliport, on 31 October 1968. The aircraft was on a training flight when it suffered a mechanical failure. The port undercarriage member became severed during the crash. Fortunately none of the crew was injured and 'WFX was taken away from the scene by crane. (*Mike Ingham*)

Dan-Air London's Airspeed AS.57 Ambassador G-AMAH at Newquay during the 1969 holiday season. The company operated a Gatwick-Newquay route that year, formerly flown by British Eagle. However, Dan-Air employed comparatively elderly Dakotas and Ambassadors rather than the Viscounts and BAC 1-11 previously flown by British Eagle. The route did not prosper and, at the end of that summer, it was discontinued. Dan-Air flew six Ambassadors over the 1969 season and G-AMAH soldiered on until March 1971, when it was finally withdrawn from use. (*Barry Cole*)

Viscount 814 G-AZLP of British Midlands Airways at Newquay during April 1970. That year, services to Newquay were flown from Birmingham, East Midlands, Glasgow and Manchester during the summer months. British Midland operated an increasing number of BAC 1-11s by that time but these were often used for the growing inclusive tour charter market, leaving the domestic links more for the Viscounts, though aircraft were moved from route to route as circumstances dictated. (R.C.B. Ashworth)

Beagle Airedale G-ARYZ of Executive Air at Baginton attempted a cross-wind landing on a wet grassy runway at St Mary's on 9 April 1970, after Auster G-AKXP had earlier blocked the preferred runway with a collapsed undercarriage. The Airedale skidded and overran into the unforgiving wall at the end of runway. Fortunately, no-one was hurt in either incident that day. (Frank Gibson)

# Six

# Military Flying: 1945-1970

Coastal Command Shackleton MR.1 'R' of 42 Squadron based at St Eval was used to transport visiting dignitaries to the station during the summer of 1953, though, as often is the case on the north Cornish coast, the weather does not reflect the particular season! Shackletons served at St Eval from November 1951, at which time 220 Squadron arrived, until March 1959 when 228 Squadron disbanded there. (*Author's collection*)

St Eval held a Battle-of-Britain Parade during September 1946. Between the massive C Type hangar Nos 2 and 3, the servicemen and women gather for the ceremony. The photograph was taken from the roof of the station's watch office. (*Via R.C.B. Ashworth*)

St Merryn hosted a disparate collection of aircraft during its lifetime. Here, a Miles M.25 Martinet TT.1, spotted during 1947. The aircraft's target towing apparatus is visible to port, mounted below the rear cockpit. The Martinet was used widely by the Fleet Air Arm's Fleet Requirements Units from 1943, serving with fifteen squadrons. Of these, however, only 725 Squadron used the type at St Merryn and only until December 1945. It is likely that this example belongs to the St Merryn Station Flight. (*Peter H.T. Green*)

Seafire F17 SX180, caught at St Merryn during 1947. The F17 mark of the Seafire was initially constructed with a standard fuselage that later gave way to a cutaway arrangement with bubble canopy as seen here. Seafires were used by St Merryn's 736 Squadron at the time this photograph was taken, though SX180 is not wearing the station's code of the period, JB, and may be a visitor. (*Bob Partridge*)

Over the summer of 1949 aircraft of the Aircraft Torpedo Development Unit, stationed at Gosport, called at RNAS Culdrose. They included (left) Fairey Swordfish II NF389 and another, accompanied by a Fairey Barracuda (right). Fortunately NF389 was saved from destruction on its retirement from active service, being transferred from the ATDU during March 1953 to RNAS Lee-on-Solent. It subsequently joined the Royal Navy Historic Flight based at RNAS Yeovilton. (*RNAS Culdrose*)

On 28 June 1949 the Culdrose Station Flight Sea Otter RD893 was obliged to make a forced landing in a field at Trenethick Barton Farm, near Helston. The aircraft nosed over on the uneven surface and came to rest inverted. Its sting-type arrestor hook dangles forlornly from the rear, while a solitary propeller blade remains attached. The hull planing bottom seems reasonably intact although the main undercarriage is in the retracted position. *(Keith Lee)*

Culdrose Mosquito T.3 VT638 452/CW of 762 Squadron crash-landed in a field just south of the station's perimeter on 19 October 1949. The cause of the crash was the starboard engine, which failed at 800ft while its port counterpart was already feathered, during a single-engined landing exercise. The station's buildings can be seen in the background. *(RNAS Culdrose)*

No.796 Squadron served at St Merryn between 1947 and 1950 as an Aircrewmans' School, at the time when the Firefly FR.1 was employed. Nearest to the camera is PP484 287/JB, the tailcode indicating St Merryn until replaced by MF in 1950. Nearly all the aircraft are equipped with ASH radar mounted in pods beneath the nose, while two distinct colour schemes are in evidence and two examples sport colourful spinners. The Squadron transferred to Culdrose in February 1954 and was finally disbanded there on 1 October 1958. (*Author's collection*)

A St Eval Open Day, probably during 1951. To the left is a Halifax, a Met 6 of 224 Squadron while, in the foreground, a Vampire is closely admired by the crowd – imagine attempting to touch the aircraft at a present-day air show where leading-edge technology is on display. The Vampire's markings are mostly obscured, but it appears to be sporting a B Conditions identity which could indicate it is an export FB.52 example. In the background is a Transport Command Hastings – altogether, quite a mixture. (*Author's collection*)

The AOC's inspection at St Mawgan during July 1952. Air Vice-Marshal T.T. Trail CB OBE inspects the Guard of Honour. In the background is the station's tower. By that time St Mawgan had been repopulated by the RAF following its abandonment after the war, the principal user being the Lancaster MR.3s of the School of Maritime Reconnaissance, fitted with ASV radar and used in a training role. (*Via R.C.B. Ashworth*)

No.778 Squadron, based at Culdrose between November 1951 and July 1952, was equipped with Skyraider AEW.1s. The aircraft employed the General Electric-produced AN/APS-20 search radar installed in a large ventral radome, for the detection of shipping and low-flying aircraft to a range of some fifty nautical miles. Here is WT968 303/CU on display at Culdrose, revealing its wing-folding arrangement, and the installation of the radome which gave an uninterrupted view within the lower hemisphere. (*Author's collection*)

Lancaster MR.3 SW283 of St Mawgan's School of Maritime Reconnaissance. The ASV radar is situated in the ventral radome, the unit's badge beneath the cockpit. The SMR Lancasters soldiered on until September 1956 when the unit made its final public appearance at the station's Battle-of-Britain open day. That month the School was disbanded and the last Lancaster was withdrawn from the RAF's strength. (*Author's collection*)

During the hard winter of 1955 experienced even in Cornwall, the Bristol Sycamore HR.12s based at St Mawgan with the Air Sea Warfare Development Unit helped deliver animal foodstuffs to remote parts of the county. This is WV781 Z-F on a snow-covered Bodmin Moor during February 1955, an area that can be exceedingly bleak in poor weather. The crew unload hay, while a number of animals can just be seen in the distance. (*Author's collection*)

Shackleton MR.1A WG510/B of 206 Squadron at St Eval during 1955. The aircraft is seen on the northern peritrack by St Eval's church. Though much of the village of St Eval had been subjected to compulsory purchase orders to make way for the airfield and then demolished, the ancient church was spared and sat within the boundary of the station. During the war, the local civilian worshippers had been issued with passes allowing them to visit. *(Via R.C.B. Ashworth)*

No.765 Squadron, based at Culdrose, operated Firefly T.2s between February 1955 and March 1957, as a Piston-Engined Pilot Pool squadron. Nearer the camera is 724/CU accompanied by another, while the Lizard peninsula forms the backdrop. 724/CU is piloted by Lt M.P. Smith with the Squadron's Staff Officer, Peter Seaborn, in the back seat. The second aircraft is piloted by Sub Lt J.T. Lyon RNVR. *(Peter Seaborn)*

No.765 Squadron personnel photographed at Culdrose during 1956-1957. Back row: Electrical Officer; Staff Officer Peter Seaborn. Front row: Engineering Officer; Lt Percy Morris, senior pilot, IR instructor and examiner; Lt Cdr David Winterton, Commanding Officer; Lt Cdr Brown, Twin QFI; Lt John Webster; and Mr 'Knocker' White. Subsequently, Morris became a Lt Cdr and White a Sub Lt. The Squadron was disbanded on 25 March 1957. (*Peter Seaborn*)

Shackleton MR.2 WR953 of 228 Squadron caught taxying at St Eval on 28 May 1956. The aircraft was in the process of transporting the then Under Secretary of State for Air, Christopher Soames, to the station for a short visit. Behind the marshal, a car waits in the background to pick up the honoured guest. (*Author's collection*)

In September 1956 the School of Maritime Reconnaissance at St Mawgan was absorbed into the Shackleton OCU at Kinloss and the RAF's last Lancasters were withdrawn. On 15 October, the final example, RF325 H-D, left St Mawgan for Wroughton and a sad trip to the breakers. (*Keith Saunders*)

Firefly T.7 WJ202 764/CU served with 796 Squadron between June 1953 and December 1957; the type was gradually replaced by the Gannet AS.1 and T.2. The Squadron served at Culdrose between February 1954 and October 1958. The Firefly T.7 differed significantly from earlier marks. It featured a revised wing planform, a beard radiator, an enlarged rear cockpit housing two radar operators, and a larger fin and rudder than previously. The external ASH radar equipment was situated in the starboard underwing pod and, because the aircraft was not intended to operate from carriers, unlike earlier Fireflies, no arrestor hook was fitted. (*Author's collection*)

RNAS Culdrose's Gannet ECM.6 XA459 394/CU. This aircraft served with 831 Squadron that operated the type between February 1961 and May 1966. During that time the unit was very nomadic but spent several periods at the Cornish station. The ECM.6 variant of the Gannet was used in Electronic Counter Measures activities and 831 Squadron operated a mixed bag of aircraft in that role, including Avenger AS.6s and Sea Venom ECM.21s. *(R.C.B. Ashworth)*

Gannet AS.1s CU/783 and CU/778 of 796 Squadron taxying at Culdrose during 1957-1958. To the left is one of the Squadron's Sea Balliols, ex-765 Squadron and employed as part of the Piston Engine Pilot Pool resource. These two types were the last to serve with 796 Squadron, which disbanded at Culdrose on 1 October 1958. *(RCPS Research Project)*

Gannet T.5 XG883 451/CU of 849 Squadron based at Culdrose. Unlike the anti-submarine versions of the aircraft, the T.5 carried no ventral radome and was a dual control trainer variant, the second set of controls being located in the observer's cockpit. No.849 Squadron operated both the Gannet T.2 and the T.5, the latter sub-type surviving in service until January 1976. (*Author's Collection*)

The Airborne Early Warning Gannet differed radically from earlier versions, introducing a completely new fuselage, fin and rudder. The large ventral radome contained the AN/APS.20 radar and was scalloped to allow sufficient clearance for the main undercarriage to retract. This AEW.3, XL456 413/CU, served with 849 Squadron at Culdrose and elsewhere, though here it carries the Culdrose station tailcode CU. The Squadron operated Gannet AEW.3s between February 1960 and December 1978. (*Author's collection*)

St Mawgan's annual Air Days, when the station is open to the public, have been popular for many years, though the north Cornish weather patterns have not always been kind to the event. No.226 Operational Conversion Unit's Lightning T.4 XM996 was present for the 1964 Air Day, its colourful scheme featuring a red spine, red and white fin and a white rudder. At that time the unit was based at RAF Coltishall. Behind the Lightning is a Hunter. *(Keith Saunders)*

The 1965 St Mawgan Air Day was attended by two McDonnell Douglas F-101A Voodoos of the United States Air Forces in Europe (USAFE) 81st Tactical Fighter Wing based at Bentwaters/Woodbridge, which were shown statically. This unit was the only Wing to operate the dedicated fighter variant of the Voodoo outside the United States. Nearer the camera is 0-41484, accompanied by 0-41473. *(Keith Saunders)*

No.626 Gliding School (later 626 Volunteer Gliding School) was formed at St Eval on 1 June 1958 but became based at Culdrose in 1963 and Predannack around six years later. The unit's Slingsby T.21B Sedbergh TX.1 WB980 is seen making a visit to St Mawgan during September 1966. No.626 VGS continues to provide air experience flights today, using Grob Viking TX.1s, and is still based at Predannack. *(Barry Cole)*

Culdrose-based 706 Squadron Wessex HAS.1 XS152 CU/576 on station during July 1966. No.706 operated in the role of a Helicopter Advanced Flying Training squadron, providing conversion of pilots to the type, advanced training to helicopter specialist pilots and operational flying training in the Commando role. The Squadron retained its Wessex HAS.1s until January 1971, by which time the Sea King had been adopted. *(R.C.B. Ashworth)*

The Maritime Operational Training Unit arrived at St Mawgan from Kinloss during 1965. They brought with them Shackleton T.4s, an example of which, WB822/T, is seen over the north Cornish coastline during September 1967. The T.4s were converted from elderly MR.1s and 1As to reproduce for training purposes the radio and navigation layout of the Shackleton MR.3. However, by late 1969, the first Nimrod MR.1s were joining 236 Operational Conversion Unit and the Shackleton's days of maritime reconnaissance were numbered. (*R.C.B. Ashworth*)

Graceful de Havilland Sea Devon C.20 XK896 served with 781 Squadron at Culdrose. The Sea Devon was an eight-seat light transport and the Navy operated thirteen of the type, which was often used for the ferrying of VIPs. This photograph was taken in 1968. By the time the Squadron disbanded on 31 March 1981 its complement of aircraft was a mixed bag comprising Sea Devons, Sea Herons, Wessex HU.5s and a Chipmunk. (*Author's collection*)

No.707 Squadron flew from Culdrose between December 1964, when it reformed, and May 1972, during which time it operated the Westland Wessex HU.5. This is XT458 CU-Y, photographed at the station during 1968. The Wessex HU.5 was used in a Commando role and employed two coupled 1,350shp Bristol Siddeley Gnome turboshaft engines. The Squadron's badge, a winged dagger, is applied just aft of the helicopter's main rotor. (*Author's collection*)

The Culdrose Station Flight operated fixed-wing aircraft initially but the Dragonfly helicopter entered service during the early 1950s and, by 1968, the Whirlwind HAR.9 was flown, as seen here. This is XN309 CU/590 on station, showing its bright day-glo patches. These aircraft were used for Search and Rescue activities prior to the arrival at Culdrose of the Sea King. (*Author's collection*)

Wessex HAS.3 XM870 566/CU was among the aircraft used by 700H Squadron to effect the introduction of the type into Naval service. It is seen at Culdrose during July 1968. To the right is sister aircraft 568/CU. The Wessex HAS.3 differed in appearance from earlier versions in featuring a thimble radome and a revised gearbox fairing aft of the main rotor. The first in-service operator of the new type was 706 Squadron. (R.C.B. Ashworth)

No.201 Squadron operated the Shackleton MR.3 from October 1958 until September 1970. The squadron was stationed at St Mawgan between October 1958 and March 1965, when a move was made to Kinloss. Here, Shackleton MR.3 WR986/M undergoes an inspection at St Mawgan. In the background is a second example. (R.C.B. Ashworth)

The Shackleton MR.3 Phase 3 included the unusual modification of adding two Viper 203 turbojets to the outer engine nacelles in order to add to the power available for take-off. Improved navigational equipment was also fitted. This is MR.3/3 WR977/B of 42 Squadron at St Mawgan during May 1968. The undercarriage wheels are wearing covers and the aircraft is chocked. (R.C.B. Ashworth)

No.846 Squadron Wessex HU.5 Commando carrier, XT461 CU-D. No.846 employed this type over the period July 1968 until October 1981; during that time the Squadron disbanded and reformed twice and was based at Culdrose on a number of occasions. Although the earlier Wessex Commando 1 had given good service, the HU.5 variant was more powerful and also employed a strengthened airframe to withstand the stresses of frequent low-flying missions. (Author's collection)

# Seven

# Civil Flying: Round-up

Rapide G-AHAG *Bryher* served with Scillonia Airways between April 1966 and May 1970, when the company ceased trading. It is seen passing over the glorious coastline of the Land's End. Its fuselage sides at that time advertised scenic flights and, on a clear day in Cornwall, Scillonia could really deliver! Sadly though, when the company's assets were auctioned off in May 1970, *Bryher* was sold for a meagre £205. (*Author's collection*)

Alidair was one of a variety of Viscount operators that provided services to Newquay. G-AZNH was delivered to the company in January 1975. That summer, the aircraft was employed in several charter flights from Zurich to Newquay, carrying Swiss businessmen to view the china clay works at St Austell as guests of English China Clays. (*Author's collection*)

Brymon Airways operated Britten-Norman BN2A Islander G-BAVT from Newquay between May and December 1975; this photograph was taken there in September. The aircraft was leased from Intra Airways. The Intra logo can be discerned beneath the hastily-applied Brymon sticker on the fin. (*R.C.B Ashworth*)

In March 1976 Brymon purchased and put into service the ex-British Midland Herald G-ATIG between Newquay and Heathrow. In some local quarters, the new acquisition became known as *Tigger*. However, the aircraft was soon withdrawn for modifications, Brymon leasing a British Air Ferry Herald and then a Skyline Viscount to provide cover. (*Author's collection*)

Islander G-BFNU joined Isles of Scilly Skybus during August 1984, the first example to arrive. It is pictured during 1985 outside the elderly hangar that has since been replaced. G-BFNU's Certificate of Airworthiness lapsed in August 1989 and the aircraft was withdrawn from service. Its fuselage, however, is still stored at the airfield, lashed to the back wall of one of the hangars. (*Author's collection*)

Castle Air's Agusta 109 G-HELY was acquired by the company in 1985. The company's logo is applied to the rear fuselage. Castle Air was formed in 1980, based at Trebrown, near Liskeard, commencing operations with Bell 206 G-LRII. Castle Air carries out charter flights but specialises in aerial filming, frequently working overseas and providing its own support on location with engineering, camera and mount staff, camera cars, production vehicles and fuel bowsers. Feature and television production work is undertaken as well as filming for network commercials. (*Author's collection*)

Isles of Scilly Skybus Islander G-SSKY seen at Land's End. G-SSKY joined the ISSB Islander fleet from new and is still in service today. In the height of the season as many as forty-five round trips to St Mary's are made by the fleet each day, each flight taking around fifteen minutes. From a servicing point of view the Islanders are better suited to many very short journeys than the company's turbine-powered Twin Otter. (*Author's collection*)

DHC.6 Twin Otter G-BIHO is employed by Isles of Scilly Skybus on the longer routes operated by the company beyond the boundaries of Cornwall. The aircraft is seen on the apron by the hangars at Land's End under a stormy sky during the autumn of 1993. Behind the aircraft is the airfield's control tower, the flying club and a workshop. (*Author*)

Piper PA-31-350 Navajo Chieftain G-GRAM belonged to the small local carrier Newquay Air Ltd. It was exhibited on the ramp at a damp St Mawgan Air Day during August 1993.(*R.C.B. Ashworth*)

Accidents in Cornwall are, thankfully, rare, but on 16 July 1977, SOCATA MS892A Rallye Commodore G-AZVI collided with gorse bushes at the end of the small airstrip at Polzeath, near Padstow. The pilot was uninjured but the aircraft suffered damage to the nose landing gear, flaps and propeller. Fire-fighters survey the scene, their vehicles parked nearby. Across the tranquil River Camel the stone tower built in 1832 as a shipping daymark lends an ironic slant; it was erected by the Association for the Preservation of Life and Property. (*Malcolm McCarthy*)

Reims Cessna F.337F Super Skymaster G-AZLO arrived on the British Civil Register during January 1972 and is seen at Land's End in May 1980. Behind are the old hangars, that bearing the legend 'Scenic Flights' surviving from 1937 when it was transported from Squire's Gate (Blackpool) and reconstructed by the St Just Engineering Company. The legend is a hangover from the 1960s when Dragon Rapides took tourists for short joy-rides. Both hangars have since been replaced, while 'ZLO's C of A expired in April 1982; the rear fuselage was stored for many years afterwards. (*Peter Wearne*)

Nearby holiday accommodation, golden sands and breathtaking walks along the cliff paths ensure that Perranporth airfield continues to attract visitors from around the country. Seen facing the sea at the northern end of the airfield during the 1980s is SOCATA TB.10 Trinidad G-TBXX. Behind are two large hangars used to accommodate gliders and powered gliders, which are still in use today. Following the restoration of the wartime watch tower at the southern end of the airfield during the 1990s, Perranporth's light aircraft generally use that part of the site on which to park, while the gliders remain at their northern facilities. *(Barry Cole)*

Bodmin airfield houses the aircraft of the Cornwall Flying Club. Seen at rest is the club's spruce Reims Cessna F.172 Skyhawk II G-BCZM. In the background is one of Bodmin's modern and roomy hangars, behind which are situated the clubroom and tower; the latter is housed in the upper part of a two-storey portacabin. The airfield employs two grass runways, 03/21 and 14/32. Bodmin is a friendly club where guests are made very welcome and can enjoy watching the flying – and the excellent cream teas! *(Author)*

The well-known Cessna FR.172F G-AWWU is owned by the Land's End Flying Club. For many years the aircraft has provided pleasure flights and, over the summer season particularly, is still to be seen over Cornish skies giving visitors to the county the time of their lives. The aircraft is seen during a quiet spell, its windscreen being spruced up with the aid of a hose. (Author)

In May 1979 John and Fran Fisher opened the Cornwall Parachute Centre on the St Ervan side of St Merryn, initially for a three-month trial period. In 1980 planning permission was sought for the club and in December 1987 it was finally granted. For many years the club has used Cessna 182 G-ATCX which, rather than the usual accommodation, has only the pilot's seat fitted, and employs a jump-off platform installed over the starboard main undercarriage member. The aircraft is housed alongside St Merryn's gyrocopters. (Author)

Two-seat Spitfire T.9 ML407 made the long trip from the Strathallan Collection in Perthshire to St Merryn during October 1979, where it was rebuilt in a wartime building over a six-year period and registered G-LFIX. Owned by Nick and Caroline Grace, on 6 January 1985 ground runs were commenced and the aircraft made a 'first' flight from the airfield on 16 April of that year, with Nick Grace at the controls. G-LFIX subsequently received a repaint and has become one of the best-known of the currently airworthy Spitfires, appearing at many public displays. *(Peter R. Arnold)*

The sole Whittaker MW.2 Excalibur, G-BDDX, at Bodmin airfield during taxying trials which took place over the spring of 1976. Designed by Mike Whittaker and financed by Mike Robertson of the Trago Mills retail empire, the Volkswagen-powered Excalibur was built at Bodmin but made its first flight from St Mawgan in the hands of Flt Lt Ernest Simmonds on 1 July 1976. The aircraft won the Tiger Cup for the best original design of the year at the PFA Rally held at Sywell that year but sadly the project was not pursued further. G-BDDX survives as an exhibit at the Flambards entertainments complex at Helston. *(Mike Whittaker)*

Evans VP-2 G-BTSC *Spirit of Truro* was built by the boys of Truro School between 1978 and 1980. The project was overseen by the school's head of Design and Technology, Dennis Keam, with help from Rod Bellamy, Viv Bellamy's son. Powered by a Volkswagen engine, the VP-2 was shown statically at the 1980 SBAC Show at Farnborough, as pictured here, before a first flight at Tregavethan airfield near Truro in the hands of Philip Irish, the airfield's owner. Further flights followed from Land's End before 'TSC was purchased by Mr Irish. The aircraft is still extant. *(Dennis Kearne)*

The Trago Mills SAH-1 trainer, G-SAHI, seen over the north Cornish coast during the mid-1980s. Designed by Syd Holloway at Bodmin, the SAH-1 made its first flight from the airfield there on 23 August 1983, piloted by Air Vice-Marshal Geoffrey Cairns. The SAH-1 was recognized as a technical masterpiece and its flight characteristics drew very wide praise, both from the aerospace industry by whom it was assessed and from those individuals who flew the aircraft. However, it proved impossible to commercially exploit the SAH-1 despite its great promise and the project faltered; only a handful of further examples were built. *(Syd Holloway)*

At St Merryn, long since abandoned by the Navy, the local gyrocopter flyers have continued in residence for many years. The prominent gyrocopter pilot and designer Chris Julian flew from St Merryn and lived at nearby Fraddon, where he had a gyrocopter repair workshop. Following a career in professional speedway racing, he became a glider pilot, but moved to gyrocopters and designed the Julian Wombat, the first of which, G-WBAT, made its first flight from St Merryn during the spring of 1991. Chris is seen here at St Merryn with his Benson B.8 G-ATLP, which he once said he had owned for more years than he cared to remember! (Chris Julian)

Known these days as the St Merryn Gyronauts, the St Merryn gyrocopter enthusiasts keep a collection of the tiny aircraft on station, hangared together with a workshop, and also employ a towed gyro-glider for air experience flights. They meet regularly each weekend and give a warm welcome to visits from the public. Here is G-WYZZ, an Air Command 532 Elite, under power at the airfield during August 1990. (Via Chris Julian)

Sikorsky S-61 G-BCEB has served the Penzance-Scilly Isles service since 1975, at which time the service was run by British Airways Helicopters. The route is currently flown by British International Helicopters. 'CEB is seen at the Penzance terminal under the flag of the latter operator during the mid-1990s. The lower part of its fuselage is equipped with roomy lockers that make 'CEB ideal for transporting tourists' baggage. The Penzance-St Mary's link is the only scheduled helicopter service in Britain and in excess of 80,000 passengers are flown yearly; the service has a great reputation for punctuality. (*Author*)

The Cornwall Air Ambulance service went operational in April 1987. The first such service in Britain, MBB Bö 105 helicopters have been employed, the first being G-AZTI though G-AZOR was used as a relief aircraft. Caught on station during February 1996 is the long-serving Bö 105DBS, G-CDBS, the first of its sub-type on the British register. The Air Ambulance is stationed at St Mawgan, though initially a compound was used adjacent to Truro's Treliske Hospital. (*Author*)

Also stationed at St Mawgan is the Trinity House Lighthouse Service Bölkow. Seen here at home during the mid-1990s is appropriately-registered Bö 105DBS/4 G-THLS, which is hangared with the Cornwall Air Ambulance for economies in accommodation and maintenance. The Trinity House Bölkow was formerly situated at Penzance heliport. The aircraft is used to inspect and maintain the unmanned lighthouses around the British coastline and for the transportation of fuel to those lighthouses powered by diesel generators. (*Author*)

A visitor from up-country: Slingsby T.61F Venture T.2 powered sailplane G-BUDT caught at Bodmin's pleasant grass parking area during 1997. Previously employed by the RAF as XZ563, the aircraft left the stores at Chivenor for private ownership by the G-BUDT Group, coming onto the Civil Register during 1992. The Venture is based at Eaglescott airfield, near Torrington in North Devon. (*Author*)

117

Perranporth's wartime watch tower was resuscitated during the mid-1990s. The building, positioned at the southern end of the airfield, is now used as a control tower for the light civil traffic there. A memorial erected by local groups and dedicated to service personnel when flying from Perranporth during the Second World War is situated near to the tower. (*Author*)

Land's End during the mid-1990s. An air traffic control tower has been added to the old buildings, but the foreground car (an Alfa Romeo 2000 Spider from the early 1960s) helps maintain a feeling of times past. The increasing frequency of traffic to and from the Isles of Scilly has led to the use of each side of Land's End's wide runways on a differential basis, in order to conserve the grass surface. (*Author*)

*Eight*

# Military Flying:
# Round-up

On 18 September 1970 the Nimrod MR.1 made its public debut at the Battle of Britain Air Display held at St Mawgan. The aircraft was flown at that time by 236 Operational Conversion Unit, which had arrived during the previous October, its job to convert Shackleton crews to the new type. (*Keith Saunders*)

Nimrod MR.1 XV235 was used by both 42 Squadron and 236 OCU at St Mawgan during the early 1970s. The two units operated their aircraft in a pool that shared a purpose-built common servicing system. In the boom aft of the tail is situated the Magnetic Anomaly Detection equipment. (*Author's collection*)

A miniature helicopter: a Culdrose Hiller HT.2 XS161/52 of 705 Squadron, photographed on a wet day at the station. No.705 Squadron's task was basic helicopter training for the Navy and its Hillers served for over twenty years. The first HT.1 variant arrived during May 1953, and the HT.2 was finally withdrawn from service in March 1975. The training function of the Hillers was taken over by the Gazelle HT.2, and both types frequently used Predannack as well as the main station. (*Author's collection*)

Prior to its conversion, the singular Short SC.9 XH132 was a Canberra PR.9. This aircraft was used in the development of the Red Top missile and is seen on approach to St Mawgan during August 1979. Following its active life, XH132 assumed the Instructional identity 8915 and remained at St Mawgan until it was disposed of, the nose section passing to a St Austell scrap dealer. *(Peter Wearne)*

In May 1982, the Harriers of No.1 Squadron positioned from Wittering to St Mawgan before commencing their long flight to Ascension in support of the Falklands Task Force. They are seen fitted with in-flight refuelling probes and underwing 330-gallon auxiliary fuel tanks. A total of sixteen No.1 Squadron Harriers passed through St Mawgan that month, intended for use as attrition replacements in support of the Falklands Sea Harrier force. *(Mike Retallack)*

Sea King HAS.1 XV660 595/CU was from the first production batch of fifty-six aircraft and served with 706 Squadron at Culdrose. No.706 flew the HAS.1 variant between 1970 and 1978. The Squadron's badge, a winged horse in flight supporting a dagger, is positioned just behind the cockpit. XV660 was subsequently upgraded to HAS.5 and later HAS.6 build and is currently on the strength of 810 Squadron, also based at Culdrose. (*Author's collection*)

Culdrose Sea King AEW.2A XV664 181/CU of 849 Squadron, caught just off the Lizard. The aircraft is equipped with Searchwater radar and its kettledrum-shaped Kevlar-covered radome is in the lowered position for deployment. In the airborne early warning role, the Sea King is able to detect incoming anti-ship missiles, the operational distance of the radar being over one hundred miles in all directions. The Sea King's FOD shield is equipped with de-icing strips and the IFF aerials are just visible on the port side. (*Courtesy of RNAS Culdrose*)

This Sea King is the Commando carrying HC.4 version flown by 845 Squadron, which is based at RNAS Yeovilton but regularly visits Culdrose, as seen here. The aircraft is ZD480/E, and is sporting NATO SFOR markings indicating service in the Split area of Bosnia. The HC.4 variant is minus the floatation sponsons of the ASW and AEW Sea Kings, its non-retractable undercarriage instead mounted on tiny stub wings. (*Author*)

Fleet Requirements and Air Direction Unit BAe Hawk T.1 XX315 on Culdrose's C Site. FRADU is responsible for the provision of target aircraft for Naval exercises and for the training of Naval Fighter Controllers and AEW Observers. Though FRADU is a government establishment it is run by industry, the present contractor being Hunting Aviation Ltd. FRADU has been operating from Culdrose since 1996. (*Author*)

Jetstream T.2 ZA111 574/CU is flown by 750 Squadron from Culdrose, where the unit has been stationed since September 1972. The Jetstream T.2 entered Squadron service in October 1978, replacing 750's ancient Sea Prince T.1s. The aircraft is still used in the observer trainer role and is seen over the English Channel. *(Courtesy of RNAS Culdrose)*

Photographed during the cheerless weather of the 1993 St Mawgan Air Day was No.22 Squadron's bright yellow Wessex XR504 HAR.2 search and rescue helicopter. No.22 Squadron operates as independent flights with detachments at various airfields in order to provide as wide a cover as possible, though its aircraft, now Sea Kings, are serviced centrally at the Squadron's headquarters at St Mawgan. *(Keith Butcher)*

The annual RNAS Culdrose Air Day continues to be a popular attraction for both locals and summer visitors to Cornwall. Civil and military, fixed- and rotary-wing aircraft participate both from the United Kingdom and overseas. Lynx HMA8 XZ732/670 of 815 Squadron's Operational Evaluation Unit shows off its British Experimental Rotor Programme (BERP) main rotor blades, nose-mounted passive identification device and 360° radome at the 1996 Air Day. (*Author*)

Predannack has for many years provided a final resting place for unwanted naval airframes, many from Culdrose and in particular the School of Aircraft Handling. These are sometimes employed for fire practice exercises. Here is Sea Venom FAW.22 XG698, certainly one of Predannack's more battered residents, minus engine, radar, wings – in fact nearly everything! The Sea Venoms were withdrawn from service during the early 1960s as the Sea Vixen became operational. (*Author's collection*)

The larger of St Merryn's watch towers, seen here in 1963, was among a feast of wartime buildings that survived the closure of the station. Many of the buildings are still extant and present a real jewel for those interested in airfield architecture. Several are in good repair and are used today for various agricultural, storage and commercial purposes. (*R.C.B. Ashworth*)

The last of the huge wartime C Type hangars at St Eval survived for many years after the war, while the abandoned station was used for motorcycle racing, car trials and by learner drivers. This photograph was taken during March 1981. Two years later, the hangar was dismantled. The airfield was subsequently secured by the Ministry of Defence. (*R.C.B. Ashworth*)

St Eval, October 1994, looking along the disused Runway 08/26. Numbers of wartime dispersals are still in evidence particularly at the top left where St Eval's church is also situated. To the top right is the former site of the station's C Type hangars and the domestic accommodation. The old peritrack now forms part of the road around the station. St Eval currently accommodates an HF communications system that supports NATO's EASTLANT area; some of the system antennas are in evidence. *(Via David Barnes)*

A Seafire F.17, possibly SX154, was erected as the gate guardian at RNAS Culdrose in around 1953. However, its shallow diving attitude combined with a propeller allowed to rotate in the wind, alarmed some passing drivers who, catching the aircraft in their peripheral vision, believed for a moment that it was about to crash! The aircraft is seen during the winter of 1955 when snow made a rare visit to the county. In 1958 a Hawker Sea Hawk replaced the Seafire as the Culdrose guardian. *(Courtesy of RNAS Culdrose)*

The largest of the gate guardians to be seen in Cornwall is Shackleton MR.2 WL795 at St Mawgan. Named *Mr Zebedee*, WL795 arrived from Lossiemouth on 24 November 1981, an ex-8 Squadron example having been in service since 8 September 1953. It had been planned to use WL795 for crash rescue training, but instead it was decided to preserve the aircraft. After extensive refurbishment, WL795 was put in its display position at the station on 24 April 1989, having been reconverted from AEW.2 to MR.2 configuration. Its restoration continues under the dedicated volunteers of the Cornish Aviation Society. (*Author*)

The Cornwall Aero Park, part of the Flambards family entertainment centre at Helston, hosts a number of preserved airframes. The collection was opened in 1976 and, not surprisingly, most of its exhibits are ex-Culdrose residents no longer required by the Navy. An exception, however, is Canberra TT.18 WK122, a target tug version mounting a Rushton towed target system manufactured by Flight Refuelling Ltd. This aircraft served with 7 Squadron, a target facilities unit, which was based at St Mawgan between May 1970 and January 1982 when the unit disbanded. (*Author*)